RECOGNITION

ELISSA IVY SIEGEL

New York City Books

Recognition

RECOGNITION

Elissa Ivy Siegel

© 2022, New York City Books

All Rights Reserved

Including the right of reproduction in whole or in part in any form.

Cover Design: Elissa Ivy Siegel

New York City Books

ISBN 978-1-0880-5793-3

First Edition

July 21, 2022

Elissa Ivy Siegel

Dedicated to the people who filled these pages.

Mum, Da', Nan, Gramps, Love Bug, and a simple country analyst.

Recognition

One

The United States of America

2022

The first thing she noticed was his ears.

(They weren't sticking out of anything.)

She was often attracted to unusual things about people. He had cute ears.

There was a scar on his ear that she thought seemed vaguely familiar. It was as if she couldn't quite grasp the memory of how he incurred the injury.

How on earth could she know how he got his scar, she thought!? They had never met.

Still, it was familiar.

At first glance, she felt an attraction.

He had a pleasing face.

Recognition

But she quickly put that out of her mind and went about her day.

{A note from the Author}
This is a thing we single people, or "singletons," if you will, do.
We automatically think everyone is taken.
Everyone in the world is already coupled.
Except us.
Except her.

So, in her mind he was quickly brushed aside.
Written off as "taken."
Even though there was no evidence confirming or denying that fact.
And so, weeks went by before another encounter took place.
She had all but forgotten him.

In the spirit of being completely vague:
An outside party encouraged her to reach out to him a few weeks later. She was asked to relay a message.

So, she reached out on behalf of said party.

She didn't expect a response.

The message wasn't really coming from her after all; she was merely relaying it.

But respond he did.

And their correspondence remained steady from then on.

Well, for a time anyway. *Let's not jump to the end too quickly.*

He seemed to be driving the correspondence forward, fostering it.

She followed his lead. Unusual for her.

They spoke daily, and many nights they would chat all night long. To spite the loss of sleep, it was fun, and it felt great connecting with someone so fully.

They were getting close alarmingly fast.

On several occasions he expressed how much he enjoyed speaking with her.

Recognition

How wonderfully disarming she was. He felt he could tell her anything.
It was as if they had known each other a lot longer. Years.
(Centuries.)
She agreed.

They spoke openly. Familiar and comforting.

She would never tell him this, but very early on in their correspondence, possibly the first or second time they spent the whole night chatting, she nearly ended their conversation by saying, "Good Night, I love you."
She didn't say it of course. Talk about a 'record scratching' moment.
But she did feel love for him, genuinely. Whole heartedly.
It was not an "I'm 'in' love with you" kind of love, she was sure of that, though that might have been possible in the future. And it wasn't an "I'm infatuated with you" sort of love.
It was an unconditional, true feeling of love. A close kinship.

It surprised her.

It was way too soon. She wasn't sure who created these social timelines. But whoever they were she was sure 'they' would agree that two days of speaking to each other was too soon.

She didn't love easily. Not in a romantic sense anyway. If this was indeed romantic, she couldn't say. She loved her friends and her family easily, but men - not so much. She spent the last few years writing them off. Avoiding them.

A string of bad relationships and terrible experiences caused her to step away from romantic entanglements, love, even sex. She needed a break. And she took it.

A very long break.

Now, here he is. Normally, the speed at which their relationship was progressing would scare her off; cause her to step back, pause. But this time she wasn't scared. She didn't want to run. She wasn't worried about it in the least. Their connection felt wonderful, and safe.

Recognition

It all felt right. She never experienced anything like this before in a relationship, this assuredness, not even in friendship. Certainly, never this quickly.

"Do you believe in past lives?" he asked.
"Hmm, I'm not sure. I'm the kind of girl who likes a little proof and in not having any proof in this case, I can't say."
He continued, "It's not often that I honestly feel quite so open right away with someone, but I do earnestly get that from you and that feels meaningful to me."
"I feel the same way," she said, her heart warming, "It is surprising how open I feel with you as well. Maybe we did know each other in a past life."
The proof was in the feeling.

She fell asleep this night feeling content, and at peace. As if she had been missing something; a piece of herself, that had finally been found.

Most mornings, they would message each other a "Good Morning" text.

He'd send one, one day. She'd send one the other. A message, a photo, a funny saying, all to say, 'I'm thinking of you when I wake.' And on it went.

During the day they would message about work if they had time.

Each night they'd come back together to talk, after work and after all the 'to-dos' of their lives were finished and put away for the day.

They would find each other again, to share, to learn about each other, to grow closer.

And this became their day to day.

They discussed everything. Their families, their lives, their likes, and dislikes, the losses in their lives, the wins, who they were as people. The talks could be fun and light and serious all in the same night. Shifting from one story to another.

They made plans for their individual futures.

Recognition

Some of those plans included things they'd like to do together.
Each day brought them closer.
They felt equally excited at the prospect of getting to know each other.

"If we had met in a past life," she started, picking up their conversation from an earlier date, "then who were we?"
"Oh, good question, hmm, well obviously you were some sort of Secret Agent." he started.
"Obviously," she agreed.
"And I was a mere civilian who accidently got caught up in one of your Top-Secret missions."
She smiled.
"You're likely with the CIA, or MI-5," he added.
"Definitely MI-5," she replied.
"Right, MI-5, and as you're parachuting down from a skyscraper, to attack your enemy and save all of England, looking very bad ass; I clumsily wander in - the confused,

naive American tourist, throwing a wrench into your plans," he muses.

She laughs, "go on. I'm enjoying this story."

"Instead of attacking your enemy, you swoop in and quickly handle me out of the way. Even though it's against protocol, you fill me in on the plans of your mission and recruit me to help you recapture the enemy."

"Why on earth would I break protocol and read you in on my mission? I am a far better agent than that!" she teased.

He laughed.

"You must have recognized some potential in me," he answered.

"Some potential, indeed!"

Laughing, they changed the subject and started talking about the details of their day.

Later that evening after they said their 'good nights' she thought about their conversation. She likes that he made her the 'bad ass' star of their past-life fantasy.

He'll be the star in their next life together, she thought.

Recognition

They could trade off.

Something else she would never tell him:
(To be fair, she never told anyone. She thought the thing she is about to reveal just might be, well, quite mad, frankly.)
Given the distance between them physically, living on opposite sides of the country. And given the closeness they were starting to feel with each other. Some strange things started happening to her.

She was never one who was spiritual, or 'in-tune' as other people claimed to be. She was more of a straight shooting, head strong, tell it like it is, New Englander. Practical. Logical.

The strange thing that started happening:
She could feel him with her.
At odd points in the day, often while doing very mundane things, she would feel his presence so strongly, so overwhelmingly, it caused her to look around the room, as if

searching for him. (Crazy! Though possibly crazy in the best possible way, she wasn't sure.)

She might be washing the dishes, or cooking something on the stove, and she would feel as if he was behind her. Close. She would turn around and face an empty kitchen.

These moments would come out of the blue. In many cases, she wasn't even thinking of him. But a feeling would come over her, as if he was there.

Sometimes it would stop her in her footsteps. The feeling of him would hit her, and she would pause. It was eerie and comforting in one. Unnerving in ways. Sometimes it would make her smile. Sometimes it would make her sad. Maybe she just missed him. Other times, he would send a text message moments after his presence was felt. Was it some sort of psychic connection? Again, she didn't know much about the psychic, or spiritual world. Whatever it was, she quickly realized she could conjure him up whenever she wished. If she was missing him, she not only could picture him or think of him, but she could feel him. Touch him. Feel him touching her. A hug, a light caress, a strength at her side.

Recognition

It was as if it was coming from memory. But that was impossible. They had never been together. And her imagination was not that creative.
Not creative enough to conjure him out of thin air on those mundane occasions.

And long after he was gone, she could still feel him.

Elissa Ivy Siegel

Two
England
1942

Part One

She didn't read the telegram, she just burst into tears upon receiving it.
The strength of her sobbing scared her. If she was crying this hard, somewhere, deep down, it meant he was dead.

She hadn't cried in the whole of the war until that point. Not even after everything she had seen in the Blitz. Everything she had been through.
Not a tear, until now.
She opened the telegram and read the words.
She pulled herself together and went back to work.

'Missing, presumed dead.'

Recognition

What does that mean? Could he still be found?
Alive?

He was on leave only a few months back. Four months ago, now, it felt longer.
He got off the train and scooped her up in a strong, secure embrace.
She threw her arms around him, lightly stroking the back of his head and neck.
He was holding on so tight.
In that tight squeeze, she would feel the stress and the fear melt away.
Her shoulders would relax for the first time in what felt like years.
She could finally exhale.
To rely on his strength for once, instead of always having to rely on her own.
Safe, supported, trusted. Complete.

Elissa Ivy Siegel

They had met shortly after the war began, and although they didn't know each other for very long, they fell in love, deeply. It was as if they had always known each other.
He was stationed overseas nearly immediately. Until now, the bulk of their relationship was in letters. Years of letters, and brief visits when he was allowed to return to England. Though the visits were never long enough.
Letters that were censored, and full of black ink. These letters contained their life together.
Their love.
He was fighting over there.
She was in England - fighting here. She worked in the factories. Trying to do her part. All the while dodging bombs, dealing with air raids, drills, and threats from the enemy. Constantly worrying about him. He could take care of himself, there was no doubt of that; but she worried all the same.
Sadly, if you added up all the days they got to spend with each other, it didn't even add up to a month.
War did that to love. It stole it.

Recognition

You had to grasp your time with each other whenever you could get it.

But war also created the strongest love.

Now he was back. Another short visit. Too short.

She was so happy to have him home. She didn't want to let go.

His embrace was so strong that it would often undo her. The longer he held her, the more the feelings she was good at pushing down, pushing aside, would creep to the surface.

When she started to feel undone, she would pull away.

Reluctantly, she stepped back, out of his embrace, and looked at him.

He was so handsome in his uniform.

They all were. Soldiers.

His dark hair was greying at the temples, and although her first thought was that he was too young for grey hair, she found it very attractive. Distinguished.

He wasn't a boy any longer.

None of them were. Soldiers.

He smiled. That smile.

He had a very pleasing face, she always thought.

She smiled back at him and linked her arm in his.

They walked from the train station to her small flat a few blocks down the road. Her landlady didn't allow men in the house, but they snuck in anyway. Undetected.

They talked for hours, holding each other, dancing, swaying in her one room flat, filling each other in on how their lives had been. At least giving as much detail as they could muster. It was hard to speak about, war. And with such little time between them on this visit, they wanted to focus on happier times.

As she did the washing up after dinner, he came up behind her and put his arms around her waist. She felt his strength again, supported. Close.

Everyone assumed she was 'that kind of girl'. All her girlfriends, the other soldiers - going out in social settings, as rare as they are now, she always thought people saw her as flirty. She was very friendly, big smile, big breasts, long legs, blonde hair, confident, bold personality. Men always took liberties to which they were never invited. She got skilled at fending them off. She could take care of herself. Often ending with them calling her a 'cold fish.' People mistook her confidence and her appearance to mean she was up for anything.

It wasn't true.

She wasn't even sure if he understood that she wasn't 'that kind of girl.'

Though she thought he did. He knew her.

The fact was, she wasn't experienced at all in the matter of sex. She had never cared about anyone like she cares about him. She had never been with anyone.

So, while her confidence spoke volumes to her experience, it was deceiving.

She truly wasn't sure what to do now.

How to proceed?

He would know.

She turned from the sink into his arms.

She was staring at his chest now feeling slightly shy. She had never been shy in her life; it felt foreign.

He reached up and caressed her cheek, gently taking her chin, and moving her gaze to his. She smiled. She remembered him now, familiar. She remembered that they had been here before, but had they? An odd sense of déjà vu. She put the thought out of her mind.

He leaned in and kissed her gently.

Her hands touched his chest, she moved them slowly up to his neck, and pulled him in for a stronger, more forceful kiss. Pressing into her, they fell back against the sink.

Something fell into the water that hadn't yet drained away. A splash of water jumped up and soaked the length of her back. She let out a shriek, and jumped closer to him, pushing them further into the room. Unlocking their embrace, they looked at each other and started to laugh.

Leave it to her to do something goofy during an incredibly romantic moment, she thought.

He grabbed a towel and tried to dry her off.

Recognition

He slowly unzipped her sopping wet dress and let her step out of it.

Standing there in her bra and slip, she looked at him and joked, "this was your plan all along, wasn't it?"

With a devilish smile he replied, "you know me too well."

Smiling, she grabbed his hand and pulled him towards her, she leaned in and kissed him long and hard. He dropped the towel and put his hands in the small of her back, gripping her securely. Pulling each other in.

They moved towards the bed. Taking his face in her hands, staring at each other for a moment, she pulled him into a hug, kissing his neck, nibbling his ear, the one with the scar. She loved his ears. Smiling to herself as she thought how silly that sounded, loving someone's ears.

She shook the thought from her mind.

Caressing the length of her back, kissing her neck, as he started to remove her undergarments. Her skin responded to his touch.

She lay on the bed and pulled him over her. His hands and mouth exploring the contours of her body.

Elissa Ivy Siegel

She was shaking. Was she nervous? No, he was familiar, trusted. Was she cold? It was freezing in the room, but she felt warm, increasingly so. And yet, her body wouldn't stop shaking.

She felt him move her legs apart, resting himself there. He was above her, surrounded by her.

He looked at her deeply now, as if checking in with her. She smiled, and caressed his arms and shoulders, drawing him closer.

She felt him enter her. Tight, as an incredible flash of heat surged through her body, she called out. The intensity of them becoming one. She moved closer to him. Her hands firmly pressed in his back, moving against him, with him, engulfing him with her love.

He had to put his hand over her mouth to muffle the sounds. The landlady might hear them. They both laughed and tried to steady themselves, quiet. They suddenly felt like kids again, hiding something from their parents.

Recognition

He removed his hand, and they looked at each other intently. His blue eyes, like hers, but different. She pulled him into her, deeper, slowly, closer. Never removing their gaze from each other.

Time passed; she wasn't sure how much time has lapsed. They were lost in each other.

His movements, strong, increasing his pace. Taking him in again and again, her back arched, her head thrust back, she grabbed onto him tightly, this feeling. It was dizzying, something was rising in her, stirring something she had never felt before. His muscles tensed, he grabbed her closer, so tightly, they felt like one. She dug her nails in, holding on. Her muscles contracted around him, overwhelming, heightened. The sound escaped from her throat; he didn't have time to muffle her screams this time. Their bodies responded in unison, together.
He collapsed on her, his full weight, completely spent.

They were both sweating even though the room was still freezing.
She was shaking again, but now she knew the cause, pure pleasure.
They lay there tangled up in each other; he was cradled in her arms, legs intertwined, pressed against each other. They fell asleep like this, feeling complete.

The next morning, she woke to the most amazing smell. Breakfast! He was at the stove cooking with his back to her. It smelled delicious. She hadn't smelled breakfast like this in years. Rations.
He turned around and smiled. Coming over to her, he sat on the edge of the bed and bent down to kiss her.
He had surprised her by getting fresh eggs, 'real' butter, sausages, fresh bread, and coffee. How he managed to find all of this she did not know. She sprung up from the bed and threw her arms around him, both laughing.
She put on her robe and joined him at the kitchen table for their feast.

As they ate, they spoke about their future. They'd be married after the war. Maybe buy a home in the countryside, close enough to London, but far enough away from the city smog. Cambridgeshire maybe.

He wanted to have at least four kids.

"Four!?" she asked.

"Definitely four," he said, smiling.

She laughed, "Ok, let's see how the first two turn out and then we'll plan from there," she added.

They laughed.

His face looked serious for a moment and then he told her an agency was recruiting him for after the war. Due to his academic standing and exemplary war record, he was the ideal candidate.

"What's sort of agency?" she asked.

"The Secret Intelligence Service."

"The SIS is recruiting you?" she clarified.

"Yes."

He was brilliant; she wasn't surprised they'd be looking at him.

Should he even be telling her this news? A feeling of loss came over her and she suddenly needed to be close to him. She reached across the table and took his hand.

Getting up from her chair and coming around the table, she sat in his lap. Curling up in his arms, pressed against his chest and resting her head on his shoulder, almost childlike. They sat like this for a long while in silence.

In this moment, she thought, silence could often be beautiful and necessary.

He lifted her and carried her to the bed; they made love and held each other until it was time to head to the station to catch his train.

Standing on the station platform in an embrace, she kissed him.

She hoped this kiss would convey all she was feeling.

That she loved him.

That she would miss him while he was gone.

Recognition

That she would worry about him until he was safely back in her arms again.

When they broke from their kiss all she said was, "thank you for breakfast!"

He laughed, "my pleasure."

The sound of the train whistle made her heart sink.

He pulled her in for one last secure embrace, and then boarded the train.

They watched each other until the train was out of sight. He from the train window, she on the platform. The sound of the train on the tracks, pulling them apart.

When the train was gone, she steadied herself, and made her way to work.

As she walked through the streets of London, she thought of their night together.

She thought of the lovely morning they had just shared.

She'll give the left-over food to her landlady when she gets home. Maybe they'll make a feast of it for dinner tonight.
She thought of him.
Four children! She recalled.
Laughing, and shaking her head, she walked into the factory for her afternoon shift.

Completely unaware that their first child was already growing inside of her.

Recognition

Part Two

Their love was rooted in something that felt utterly eternal. Majestic & Endless.

It had been some time since she had seen him last.

She sat down to write him a letter, but she felt nervous. How to begin?

What if he is not ready for this? Was she?

She wished she could do this face to face, but needs must.

The letter began:

> *Hello My Lovely,*
>
> *I hope this letter finds you safe and well.*
>
> *I wish I could see you to deliver this news in person, but here we are – letters. The written word detailing our life together.*
>
> *The big news is that you are going to be a father!*
>
> *I'm pregnant.*

I know we were not planning on starting our family quite so soon, but this little one has other plans. I've been to see the doctor and he says everything looks good.

Baby and Mum are very healthy.

I long to see you, to hold you.

Please be careful out there.

We love you!

I miss you.

Love,

Your Girl

She rushed out of the flat and headed down the street to post the letter. She already felt anxious to receive his reply.

Weeks went by. She spent her time working, having dinner and long talks with her landlady, going out with her friends from the factory. She wasn't ready to tell anyone about the baby. She was excited, and very happy. But it was tricky. They weren't married. What would she tell them? Would they all think she's "that kind of girl" again? Luckily, she wasn't showing yet. It might be a while before that happens. Thus far, she hadn't had any morning sickness, for that she

Recognition

was thankful. Her ferocious appetite was her only pregnancy symptom. It was no easy task living on rations while pregnant. She was constantly hungry. Thankfully her work at the factory kept her very fit, she hadn't put on much weight, to spite eating everything in sight.

When she got home that night, her landlady greeted her with a smile, and the mail.

His letter.

She snatched it out of her hand and ran to her room to read it, like she might have done to her mother in adolescence.

Her landlady laughed.

The letter began:

> *My Love,*
>
> *I cannot express how happy I was to receive your news. This is truly cause for celebration!*
>
> *I love you so much, and I am so excited to learn that I am going to become a father.*
>
> *I can't wait to raise this child, and all our future children with you.*

The count was four – remember!

Since I last saw you, you have been in my every thought.

You are forever on my mind, and in my heart.

I long to hold you.

I don't have my leave dates just yet, but I hope it's sooner rather than later.

Being without you is too much to bear.

I miss you, and I love you both.

Yours.

(He had drawn balloons and a bottle of champagne in the corners of the letter).

She read the letter again, her heart aching. She needed to see him, be with him.

He was right; it was too much to bear.

That would be the last letter she would receive from him.

The next piece of mail she receives is the telegram.

The day of the telegram:

Recognition

When she returned to work, after reading it, the girls were looking at her. They know what a telegram means. She could not bring herself to return their gaze, though she felt their eyes on her. She went back to the task at hand; she focused on the machinery, the conveyor belts, the sounds of the metal. Work. It was what she knew. Something she could handle. When she got home, her landlady was in the front sitting room. This was a communal space for the girls who lived in the house.

She entered the room, sat down next to her, and put her head in her lap.

Like mother and child.

She wept for a very, very long time.

She wept for her parents. She lost them in the Blitz. She didn't cry then when it happened.

She was in shock, they told her, covered in soot, blood, God knows what else. They bundled her into a truck and took her to the hospital that day. She knew they were dead; she saw it happen. All she could do at the time was stare. After she was checked over by the medical staff and discharged, she went straight to the factory and began to work. She knew how to do that. She didn't know how to do the rest: How to grieve? How to be without them?

After work the day of the Blitz, one of the girls from the factory brought her to the landlady's house, and she never left. Luckily, there was a flat available for her.

Safe there now.

She wept for her family, for her friends, the girls at the factory who had lost their husbands, families, loved ones. She thought of the camps. She couldn't imagine the suffering. It's so much loss. It started to spiral; it was overwhelming her.

She was wailing now.

The other girls came out of their rooms and surround her in the sitting room, she could feel them supporting her. One of them put a cool cloth to the back of her neck.

It helped.

She thought of him.

'Missing. Presumed Dead.'

Recognition

She couldn't stop crying; it felt like she couldn't breathe. She couldn't speak.

She fished the telegram out of her pocket and handed it to her landlady, without lifting her head from her lap.

And then they all knew.

One by one the girls slowly went back to their individual rooms.

Her landlady helped her up and walked her to her room; putting her to bed, she sat with her until she drifted to sleep, despite the sobbing.

The next morning, she could see the light coming in through the curtains. It felt late. She bolted out of bed; it was late! What happened to her alarm?

"Bloody hell!" she got up and started to get ready for work. She was never late, this is unacceptable.

Her landlady knocked on the door, and came in.

"I overslept!"

"I turned your alarm off." The landlady confessed.

"What? Why?"

"I sent one of the girls to the factory with a note. I told them you needed the day off, and that you had suffered a loss." she informed her.

Her face turning red as she blurted out, "It isn't a loss. HE IS NOT DEAD!"

(He's just missing.)

She immediately felt sorry for yelling. Her landlady has been such a great friend to her in this past year. She didn't apologize; she walked over to her landlady and gave her a hug.

"Now get dressed, and come down for breakfast, I cooked." Her landlady directed.

While they ate, she told her landlady everything. (Confession time.)

"Around four months ago, he was on leave." she started.

"I let him spend the night in my flat." She looked at her landlady for her reaction.

"Yes, I remember hearing the evidence of that particular encounter." her landlady teased.

Recognition

Her eyes widened, and her cheeks blushed. "I'm so sorry!", she giggled.

"It's fine. I know you're not one of those girls who would make a habit of it; bring several 'visitors' to the house on a regular basis."

"Besides, I know how much you love your beau." she added.

Her beau. She felt a lump in her throat, she swallowed it down and steadied herself.

"Now for the big news." she prepared her landlady.

"There's bigger news than your night together?"

"The news is the result of that night." She looked at her landlady with big soulful eyes.

"I'm pregnant."

"Ah, I see." She lowered the cup of tea she was drinking to the table.

"Well, congratulations are in order. Let us celebrate!" Her landlady got up and went to the cabinet. She removed a small bottle of sherry.

They toasted two small glasses of the liquid to wet the baby's head.

"Are you disappointed in me?" she asked her landlady.

"Heavens no, my girl! This child was made in love. There is never any disappointment in that."

"But we weren't married," she paused, "we would have been. We discussed it while he was here, the plan was to marry after the war. We thought we had time.", she explained.

"Best laid plans, my dear."

She nodded.

The rest of the afternoon was spent drinking tea and chatting about their lives.

The girls started to arrive back to the house after their long workday.

She suddenly felt very tired. She thanked her landlady, for, well, everything, then headed upstairs and went back to bed.

Spring, 1943

The last months seemed to go by in a flash.

Recognition

She enjoyed being pregnant. The girls kept telling her how lucky she was, no morning sickness, no aches and pains, no swelling, etc. She never got any of the dreaded symptoms that often-accompanied pregnancy.

A few months back, when she started showing and couldn't hide it any longer, she was moved to a desk job. Though she missed being on the factory floor, she was grateful to be off her feet.

It had been a good day at the office this day. She had gotten the payroll accounts done and she was hoping to head home early today to meet the girls at the house. They were having a small celebration for her landlady's birthday. Her landlady had done so much for her, for all of them, over the years. She really was like a mum to us all, she thought.

Earlier in the day she had "one of those moments." Those eerie moments when she feels him close to her. It's as if he is there. They'd come over her from time to time. She never told anyone about these moments. They used to scare her. But now she just accepts them. Welcomes them.

In any case, he's here with her today.

She got up and walked down the stairs to the factory floor. She needed to get one last signature from her colleague to complete her paperwork, and then she would be done for the day.

As she got to the bottom step, her water broke. She was standing in a puddle.

Unsure of what to do for a moment, she looked around. One of the women was rushing towards her to assist.

"Come on love, take a seat here on the step." The woman tells another girl to call the medical staff.

"Don't worry love, you stick with me, I've done this eight times myself."

"Eight times! Bloody hell!" she laughs. Then she let out a low, deep groan. The pain is sharp, and frequent. He's coming too fast. (She decided months ago - that he would be a he.)

"WHOAAAA!" she grabbed onto the woman, "is this much pain normal?" she asked.

"Oh yes love, you're doing just fine."

Recognition

She can feel the baby crowning, it's too fast. The medical staff haven't arrived yet.

The woman who was sitting beside her and supporting her back moved to the ground now. She lifted her skirt and removed her underclothing to take a look.

"This little one isn't wasting any time, love! I can see a thick, dark head of hair."

The woman left her for a moment to grab a clean cloth.

"Ok love, when you feel the pain again, I need you to push!"

Suddenly, she felt scared. She grabbed the woman's hand and gave it a tight squeeze.

And then, she felt him. He was there with her again. A strength at her side. She started to cry.

Her cries turn into a loud moan.

"Ok love, I need to take my hand back now. Your little one is ready to meet the world."

She pushed, hard. Gasping for more air. Pushing again.

"There now love, that's the head born. One more big push and you'll be able to see your baby."

One big push. She feels him fall from her. She can see the medical staff rushing over.

The woman is wiping him off and wrapping him in the cloth.

And then, a cry. His cry.

"It's a boy! You have a lovely little lad, my love."

"I know." she said, smiley.

The medical staff step in to finish up.

"You took your bloody time getting here!" the woman said, "We've already done all of the hard work." She smiled at her and gave her a wink.

She cannot stop looking at him. Her son, who now has his father's name.

He is the very image of him.

Christmas, 1945

We received an unexpected visitor this Christmas, offering gifts we could not have imagined.

Recognition

She and her son remained in her small, one room flat. She thought of getting a bigger place when he was born, but she felt safe in her flat. She was happy there with her landlady and the other girls. And while he was still small, it was more than enough space for the two of them. When he grew out of the bassinet, she bought a small bed that she placed beside hers.

He would reach his hand out towards her at night, and she'd grasp it. They would fall asleep like this. Except on those really cold winter nights, when he'd crawl into bed with her for a cuddle.

Her son and her landlady were inseparable. Shortly after he could speak, he started calling her Nana, or Nan for short. And soon, they both took to calling her Nan. It just fit. She was their family now.

This was the first Christmas after the war had ended. They wanted to make it special. Nan went overboard with the cooking, she usually did. And with the presents. All the girls living in the house loved her son. They showered him with treats and gifts the entire year long.

She told them not to go too crazy with presents this Christmas, though she knew they wouldn't listen. He was spoilt to be sure. But she loved them for it.

They were all in the kitchen helping to prepare tomorrow's feast; they barely heard the knock at the door with the music playing.

"I'll get it" she yelled to the girls over the music.

She opened the door to a man in uniform, who addressed her by name.

"Yes, that's me" she said, confused as to how he knew her.

Her son ran up from behind her and hugged her leg, peering out to see who was at the door.

The man smiled. He was looking at her son as if he knew him.

She put her arm around her son and pulled him closer.

"Who are you?" she asked.

Recognition

The man introduced himself, complete with full rank, military style. He explained that he had some documents for her to review. He said he was a close friend of her husbands.

She looked confused.

And then he said his name.

"I guess you better come in," she opened the door wider.

She sent her son off with Nan, as she led the man up to her flat, away from the music and the festivities.

They sat at her kitchen table.

"He wasn't my husband; we were never married" she confessed.

He didn't look surprised. He opened his case, took out several documents and laid them on the table.

"Before your husband went missing" he started.

She got annoyed, was he deaf?

He went on, "he put certain measures in place to ensure his family would be well provided for in life."

She listened.

"The first of which was purchasing this house in your name," he showed her the deed.

"Secondly, two bank accounts were set up, one for you and one for your son, to be handled by you until he comes of age."

"Also, I thought you should have these," he handed her their letters, the ones she had sent him over the years, their letters, containing their love.

She took the letters and held them against her chest.

"And lastly, there is this," he took out another document and laid it on the table.

A marriage certificate.

She sat in silence, her head spinning; how did he manage to do all of this?

"I don't understand?" she looked at him, "How could he afford to do all of this?"

"And what's more, that certificate can't be legitimate," she added.

"Your husband was a man of considerable means. The moment he heard you were pregnant he put these plans in place."

Recognition

She thought about their time together. She realized they had never spoken about money. She had no idea what his circumstances were, it never mattered she supposed.

"And as for the document, it is real. You are registered as husband and wife. He saw to filing the document with the registry before his disappearance," he added.

"But this has my signature on it; I never signed such a document" she protested, "it's a forgery."

The man paused, looking at her for a moment.

"He thought it would be easier," he tried to explain.

Getting annoyed again, she said, "easier for WHO!?"

"Easier for your son."

She paused. Her anger subsiding, she could see the thought behind it now. He did this so his son wouldn't be labeled a bastard.

Her heart ached.

"I see" she whispered.

"I'm sorry for yelling" she said to him.

"It's quite alright. He had spoken of you often, and I feel as though I know you. He said you were fiery," he confessed.

She laughed.

He smiled.

"This is all too much. We don't need all of this," she went on.

"You may need it as your son grows older. And it is the house you two spoke about purchasing after the war," he handed her the deed so she could take a closer look.

It was in the village just outside of Cambridge, their quaint little countryside home, on the green, complete with a view of the river.

She began to cry.

"I'm sorry," she dried her eyes.

The man went on. He explained that he had tried to bring the documents to her sooner, but he himself was wounded in the war, and had been convalescing these last years overseas. This was the first chance he had to bring her the information. He went on to explain how close he and her husband were, the best of friends, and expressed how much he missed his old friend.

"Were you with him?" she asked, "before he… disappeared."

Recognition

"Yes, we were on the same assignment, though shortly before the operation took a turn for the worse, we were separated. It was then that I was wounded," he explained.

She nodded.

"And he was never found?" she asked, even though she knew the answer.

"No."

For years, after the telegram, she would insist, "he's not dead, he's just missing."

But somewhere along the way she stopped trying to convince people, stopped trying to convince herself. For her, he wasn't dead, he wasn't missing, he just simply wasn't there anymore.

She thanked him and invited him to stay for the pre-Christmas feast they were cooking downstairs.

"Oh, I couldn't possible intrude," he said politely.

"Don't be daft! There's nothing these girls would like more than to have a handsome soldier join us for dinner" she joked.

He blushed and accepted the invitation.

She brought him downstairs and introduced him to Nan and the girls.

Her son, who was never shy, ran up and hugged the man. He bent down and lifted the boy high up in the air and settled him on his waist. Her son squealing in delight as he was scooped up, nestled his face in the man's neck and shoulders.

She smiled, though it pained her a bit. Perhaps her son needed more male role models in his life. She wasn't sure how she was going to cope, having to be both mum and dad. She knew she would fall short somewhere along the way.

Nan came up next to her and grabbed her hand, giving it a squeeze.

She nodded and smiled.

Recognition

A wonderful time was had by all during their little dinner party.

Truly a time to celebrate.

Elissa Ivy Siegel

Three
The United States of America
2022

In the first few weeks of knowing each other she only thought of him as a friend. It wasn't that she didn't want more. She did. But she thought it was just a good friendship occurring here, and nothing more. She didn't believe he wanted more.

Singletons are often slow to the mark.

Then something shifted, and they were suddenly talking about more.
The conversations became intimate in nature.
The walls she had built around her, like bloody Fort Knox, came down.
She started to believe they could have more.
He admitted to wanting more.

Recognition

She started to feel more.

And then he left.

The odd thing was, she never told anyone about him.

It was as if he didn't exist, not so far as her friends and family were concerned.

The people in her life had no clue that he was even in the picture, albeit for a short time.

A ghost.

She didn't tell anyone for a few reasons:

One. During the more exciting times of getting to know each other, back when they were speaking, nearly everyone else in her life was going through hardships in their personal lives. So, her friends would call her to vent about their troubles, and it felt very shallow to take that all in and then turn around and say, "well anyway, sorry your world is falling apart, but I met a great guy that I'm really excited about!" It just didn't flow.

Two. It was over too quickly. It was essentially... nothing. Though she thought it was something. But it was nothing. (She goes back and forth with this one – something/nothing.) In any case, by the time she had the opportunity to share the reality of him, it was over.
Nothing to tell.

Three. She had some idiotic, foolish hope that he might return one day.

A few weeks later, while touring through England and Scotland, she told her friend about him. Though she was incredibly vague. She didn't have the strength to go into detail.
While riding on the train from London to Cambridge her friend asked what she had been up to in the last few months.
"Well, I met a guy."
Her friends' face lit up.
"No, don't get excited, he's already gone."
"Oh, no, what did you do!?" he asked.

Recognition

She laughed. She knew what he meant. She was often very salty by nature. Though as her friend would say, "you're a straight up BITCH." She knew it was true. And she made no apologies.

"Believe it or not, I was actually nice this time."

They laughed.

"I can tell you really liked him," he said, "when you speak of him you get a twinkle in your eye that I've never seen before."

"What!? No, I don't! SHUT UP!" Then she put her sunglasses back on.

He smiled and tried not to push her to say more. He gave her a moment.

Sometime later, "so, what happened?"

Pushing her sunglasses to the top of her head, she said "ultimately, nothing happened. We met, we talked, I thought we were getting close… I thought there was a real connection between us, and then he disappeared without a word."

"WHAT!?" he exclaimed "he never said anything?"

"Nope, he completely ghosted me," she informed. "He sent some very sweet messages the morning he disappeared; he asked me to contact him when I got home from work later that day, which I did, and then I never heard from him again."

Her friend looked confused.
"What a fucking asshole!?" he blurted out.
She laughed, "I'm not even mad. It's just disappointing. I thought he had more integrity than that, but I was wrong. I also thought he could tell me anything, so to go from constant communication to complete silence seemed out of character. But I'm not angry with him; he's free to do as he wishes."

(She thought about his silence. It was cruel. Cold.)

"Anyway," she said, "it didn't amount to much."
Her friend looked wounded, as if he was insulted on her behalf. "I hate people."

Recognition

She nodded, "well, you know the saying, 'one swallow does not a summer make'".

"Who said that? Is that sexual?"

She laughed, "leave it to you to make it so."

"It was Aristotle," she went on, "I just mean… it was one brief happy encounter, but it's over, I made too much of it."

They sat back and continued to watch the lovely view from the train window.

One the plus side, their day in Cambridge could not have been more fantastic!

She had always loved that area, she thought. Though this was the first time she had visited.

She shook her head; she really is losing it now.

This place, like him, felt unusually familiar.

Four

Scotland

1852

She wasn't royalty, well not really. There was some discussion about a blood line, but she was so far down in the line of succession that she didn't consider herself a true 'royal'.

Her 'Mother' considered them royalty, but luckily her Da' was more down to earth like his daughter. As she passed by them in the sitting room, she could hear her mother going on and on about the prince purchasing Balmoral for the Queen, and how incredibly romantic it was.

"Bye Mum, I'm going out for a walk," she yelled passing by.

"Call me "Mother", it's more ladylike."

Her daughter rolled her eyes.

Da' smiled and gave a wave.

And she was off, nearly racing out of the house, down the path, and towards the loch.

Recognition

It was a gorgeous day. The sun beautifully shone this day, she thought.

Traveling along the water, she broke off and headed into the woods that lined her family's property. She had played there when she was young; she knew the grounds like the back of her hand. One of her favorite spots was just ahead. The woods opened to a clearing on a hill that offered a beautiful view of the loch.

As she emerged from the tree line, she was knocked to the ground. Hard.

It took her breath from her, and she struggled to steady herself and understand what just happened. He was lying on the ground next to her.

Are men falling from the sky now, she wondered?

'Mother' would be pleased.

Her mother had been playing matchmaker. Making it her full-time commitment to find her daughter a suitable partner. Suitable, by 'Mother's' standards was someone of "good birth", "healthy means", and "titled".

Elissa Ivy Siegel

Her daughter: eye roll.

She looked at him again. Was he ok?

"Are you ok?" he asked.

"What happened."

"I fell out of the tree," he said, "you broke my fall."

"Happy I could oblige," she said, as she sat up rubbing the back of her head. She had hit the ground very hard.

"Did you hurt your head?" He looked at her with real concern now. He had kind eyes, and a sweet face. Very pleasing indeed.

"I'll be alright, it's just a small bump."

He stood up and offered her his hand. She accepted it and rose to her feet.

She introduced herself and informed him that this was her father's land.

"Ah, so this is 'your' family land?"

He seemed to know her family name, or at least had heard of them.

"Why were you up in the tree?" she asked.

Recognition

"I was trying to get a better view of the land; it is for my work," he informed her.

She nodded.

At this, he bowed and said, "I am a simple country analyst, m'lady."

She laughed. Not at his profession, but at the way he said it, with the bow and the 'm'lady.'

He smiled at her. Somehow, he knew she wasn't laughing 'at' him.

"We can dispense with the formalities," she offered.

She looked at his gear, a tent wrapped up, some cookware, a change of clothes.

"Are you living on the land while you work?" she asked.

He looked worried for a moment.

"Oh, it's ok, my Da' won't mind," she added. "I was just curious."

"Yes, I travel from territory to territory surveying the land for The Crown. It often results in many nights slept under the stars and living off the land."

She found this fascinating. All she ever wanted to do was travel the world. See far off lands. Granted, he was doing this locally throughout England, Scotland, and Ireland, but it was still exciting to her. It sounded like total freedom. She was eager to hear all about it.

"Come home with me and have dinner with us tonight," she invited.

"Oh, I couldn't possibly impose."

"It's no imposition. Mum has had Cook stirring up a feast all day, and it is far too much food for us to eat; we're a small family. Please, join us. That is of course, if I can tear you away from your treehouse," she joked.

He smiled.

She could feel the Haar creeping in over the loch. A chill went through her.

She reached out her hand, and in taking his, she led him back to her house without waiting for his response.

He allowed himself to be led.

Recognition

Da' couldn't have been more pleased. He was grateful to have the company and enjoyed talking with him. Someone new to speak to, some male companionship.

They spoke about business at first. The Country Analyst was in the area specifically to survey her uncle's land, which ran alongside their property.

Her uncle had died several months ago. It still pained her. She had been close to her uncle; he was like a second father of sorts.

He was explaining that the land would revert to The Crown, unless her Da' wanted to purchase it.

Mother would have preferred they purchased the land, though Da' didn't know why?

They had more than they needed with their own land.

Da' told him as much. He had no interest in obtaining more land.

Mother made a 'tutting' sound.

They all ignored her.

Over dinner, which was plentiful, and delicious (Cook was a genius in the kitchen), the Country Analyst told them of his travels and the extent of his work. She and Da' hung on his every word.

It all really did sound fascinating.

Mother kept her eye on her daughter. She wasn't happy with the look she saw in her daughter's eye when she looked at him.

Even more disturbing, this boy seemed to be looking at her daughter in the same way.

It couldn't be love surely. They'd only just met. But they were looking at each other, deeply.

There was a familiarity between them that took most couples years to build.

Mother frowned.

Da' invited him to stay on while he finished his work in the area. This invitation pleased his daughter immensely.

The Country Analyst looked shy for a moment, he looked at Da' and her, and smiled.

Recognition

Then he looked over at her mother. She was quiet, for once (biting her tongue).

Da' must have spoken to her before he offered the invitation, his daughter thought. Mother was never quiet.

"Stay," she requested.

"Thank you for the generous invitation," he said to her da', "I will stay."

She smiled.

Mother frowned again.

Da' put his arm around him and showed him to his chambers.

He stayed for the remainder of the summer.

He would go out each day to complete his work. And at night they'd come together to talk and get to know each other better. They'd often go for long walks along the loch or go swimming in the pond. It was a glorious summer.

Mother griped the whole time. Though if her mother was honest, she did like this boy. She liked everything about him, except his station in life. He wasn't a Lord. He wasn't Royalty.

He was "a simple country analyst".

"What the hell does that even mean!" her mother started.

"Oh, leave them be Mother, they're in love," her father explained.

"Love!? Pish. What do you know, you're just a man!" Mother spat back.

He didn't know how to argue this statement, so he just shrugged.

"I think he's good for her," he started again.

"And how do you come to that conclusion?" Mother insisted.

He began to tell her something he witnessed a few weeks back. He had been observing the couple at the market one day. His daughter was clearly about to verbally attack one of the merchants. She often lost her temper, especially if she witnessed an injustice, or thought she was being taken for a fool. She was fiery, indeed, and quick to put people in their place.

Recognition

But just as she was about to give this merchant a right dressing down, the Country Analyst put his hand on her arm. A small gesture. But it defused her temper. She eased off, and they walked away.

Her Da' looked at them and thought they were perfectly matched.

It wasn't that this boy was the water to her flame. No, her flame could not be dampened.

He was also a flame. Two flames, burning bright, matched in strength and passion.

Her Da' laughed then, if or when they ever fight, they'll tear the house down! But if they get it right, as he believes they will, their flames will fuel them, holding them in strength and light.

Two flames, understanding, and recognizing each other.

This time Mother didn't know what to say, a rarity indeed. She just shrugged.

Not remaining quiet for long, she piped up, "I'm glad the three of you are enjoying this wee romantic fantasy, but the fact remains that very soon, at the close of the summer, this boy is going to go back to wherever he came from, and our daughter is going to be left heartbroken."

Da' frowned. He hadn't thought of that.

Mother always loved being right. Except in this instance.

The summer did indeed come to an end, and alas, they were saying their goodbyes.

Da' started, "safe travels my boy! You know you're welcome here anytime. Come and visit us again soon."

Mother stepped towards him and handed him a parcel she organized with Cook. It contained everything but the kitchen sink. Da' wondered how the boy would carry all that food.

Mother gave him a light kiss on the cheek, "take care of yourself, love."

He was a little surprised, he always assumed her mother hated him. (It was only half true.)

"Thank you both for everything this summer," he told them.

Recognition

Her parents headed back in the house to give them some privacy.

They walked along the loch, and up to their favorite spot, where they first met.
When he nearly knocked her out by landing on her, she would always tease.
They sat on the side of the hill and looked out over the water.
He took her hand in his, and they sat there for a long while in silence.
They understood what the other was thinking. Somehow, the silence said it all.
When you love someone, everything is understood.
After a time, they got up and he prepared to go.
He pulled her in and kissed her.
It wasn't their first kiss, which happened shortly after he had arrived at the start of the summer. Though, standing here on the very same spot, she hoped this would not be their last kiss.

He turned to go, and she watched him walk down the path. He gave her one last wave, and then disappeared in the tree line.

The Haar was rolling in again; she wrapped her shawl around her, and hurried home.

Standing in the doorway, her parents were waiting for her, staring at her intently, as if they expected her to break.

"Well?" Mother asked.

"He said he would write. Let's see if he does, shall we?" she replied, smiling, and happily running off to the kitchen to help Cook prepare the dinner.

"She seems ok," Da' said.

"She's stronger than we thought," Mother said, "if he doesn't write, she'll be fine, no cause for any heartbreak. But if he does write, it will only lead to trouble."

"How do you figure that? Surely writing her is the desired outcome?" Da' asked.

Recognition

"She is fine now without him. But if he writes, and they continue to get closer, she might not be able to let go when they're deeper into their courtship. It's better if he leaves now full stop."

Da' thought about this backwards logic, and decided his wife was right.

She usually was in the end.

Some weeks later his first letter arrived.

And it began: courtship.

"The boy wrote to her," Mother began, "she snatched the letter out of my hand and ran upstairs to read it in her room. She came down sometime later looking all starry eyed, flushed, and smiling."

"This is a good thing, isn't it?" Da' asked.

"How many times do I have to explain this to you!" Mother spoke, "what could really come of this courtship? He travels all over the country, "analyzing", he won't be back this way for God knows how long, and this, being the nature of his job, will continue indefinitely."

"If they're in love they'll find a way to be together," Da' mused.

Mother shook her head at him. She gave up.

The letters continued steadily. This courtship was in full swing.

Her daughter seemed pleased and very content with the arrangement. The letters kept him near, even if he was physically far away.

He'd tell her all about his travels and the visits to the other properties. He often told her that people weren't always as friendly as her Da'. He rarely got such a warm welcome when surveying their lands. But for the most part, work was going well.

She would fill him in on the life in the village, the goings on at the market, and how Da' and Mum were doing.

They always expressed how much they missed each other and hoped to see each other soon.

Recognition

But the weeks turned into months, and Mother could see that not being able to see him was starting to wear on her daughter.

"I've decided to have a soiree," Mother began.
"Oh no, what is this in aid of?" Da' asked.
"She needs some cheering up. And it's about time she met someone else. A suitable partner."
"Oi, don't start your matchmaking again! She likes this boy, leave her be," Da' pleaded.
"This boy may never return. It has been nearly a year since he left this house last summer!" she argued. "And it's starting to trouble her, she isn't as cheery as she once was when the letters first started to arrive."
Da' shrugged. "Ok, have your party."
"It's a soiree."
Da': eye roll.

Mother and Cook went into full party planning mode.
(Soiree planning mode.)

They spared no expense, they ordered and planned all the decorations and flowers, they invited all the guests, especially the eligible young men near and far, and the food was to be a triumph.

Da' and daughter basically stayed out of the way until the day of the event.

Mother had taken her to buy a new dress for the occasion a few weeks back, and although these soirees weren't really her cup of tea, her daughter was looking forward to it.

The day of the event:

People seemed to arrive in large crowds. How many people did her mother invite? It was the soiree of the century! That is what her mother told everyone anyway.

"Mum where are all my girlfriends?" her daughter asked.

"Call me 'Mother'! I didn't invite them, it's too much competition having too many young ladies about the place," her mother informed her.

Eyes wide, "Mother! Too much competition?" she looked at her Da'.

Recognition

He just shook his head.

"You are calculating old woman! Calculating!" she teased her mother.

Da' laughed.

Her mother waved her away with the flick of her wrist, "go and mingle."

She obeyed.

Understanding that her friends wouldn't be attending this evening, she looked around the room, wondering where to begin. Wall to wall eligible bachelors. Leave it to Mum.

The music began, and Bachelor #1 stepped toward her and asked her to dance.

She looked over at her mother, she looked pleased as punch.

She took Bachelor #1's hand and was led to the dance floor.

The night continued like this, Bachelor #2, Bachelor #3, 4, 5, 6…

Dance after dance.

On any other occasion, she would be flattered to have such a full dance card. But being the only young lady at the soiree does somewhat dampen the flattery.

Soon after, dinner was served, and everyone seemed to be having a lovely time.

All in good spirts.

As the dessert was served, the dance floor started up again.

She was hoping to sit this one out.

Bachelor #10 or 11, she can't remember, sat down next to her. She looked at him and smiled. He was attractive, and he seemed very sweet. It was nice to sit and talk for a change. The dancing was getting monotonous.

Mother perked up, and jabbed Da' in the ribs, "look, she like's this one!"

"How do you know woman!? They're clear across the room!"

"I know."

"Look at how she looks at him, she sees some potential there," Mother added.

Da' looked over at them. "Maybe."

Recognition

A considerable amount of time went by, they had had a nice chat, and then she excused herself and walked out onto the balcony for some air.

He was nice, she thought. Easy to talk to in any case.

She looked out at the loch and let her mind wander. She wasn't quite ready to go back in just yet, it had been a long night, and the air felt good. It was getting too stuffy in there.

Lost in thought, she didn't hear him come up behind her. He put his arm around her waist and pulled her in.

Startled at the thought of which Bachelor this could be, she turned around abruptly.

It was him, her simple country analyst.

She smiled and jumped into his arms for an embrace.

"Your Da' let me in, he told me you were out here," he smiled.

She kissed him, long and hard. She hadn't realized how much she missed him until she saw him. He was nearly out of mind.

"Bloody typical!" her mother spat.

"Mother!" Da' said trying to calm her down.

"Well, it is typical of men. The moment she has her eyes set on someone else, he returns."

"TYPICAL!" she added one last time.

"Alright, alright. Let them be. She's happy that he's back," Da' said.

"And just how long is he staying this time?" Mother inquired.

"He says he'll be stationed here for some time, at least until next June or July. So, it's a good long while this round."

"And I suppose you invited him to stay here?" she asked.

"Of course."

Tut.

She loved this time of year, Autumn. The cool, crisp air, the change in color in the leaves, the smell of the earth. As they all settled in at the house they started to become a true family of sorts. He was included in everything, the holidays, family functions, he even helped Cook in the kitchen.

One evening when daughter and Da' were heading out for one of their long walk and talks they invited him to come along.

"I'm going to stay here and keep your mother company," he told them.

Daughter and Da' looked at each other.

"Good luck to you, my boy!" Da' said.

And they all laughed.

"What are you laughing at?" Mother called from the sitting room.

"NOTHING!" in unison.

He turned to go back in the sitting room and daughter and Da' made their way towards the loch.

This became a daily occurrence when the weather would hold.

They'd go out for their early evening walk.

He'd stay at home to keep Mum company.

And so it went.

They'd all come back together again for supper. Then he'd sit with her Da' after the meal to have a drink and talk about their day. She'd help Cook clean up, and then head to her room to write or read. Mother would be in the sitting room waiting for Da' to finish their 'guy talk'.

In the evening, The Analyst would always come to her room, and they would talk for hours.

Sometime later, Da' would check on them. He'd pop his head in from behind the door, "hello you two." It was an unspoken warning, as if to say, you better be in your own bedchamber before lights out. And then he would wish them good night.

The ebb and flow of their days as a family.

Da' and daughter never asked him or Mother what they spoke about. And they never actually said, but Mother seemed to be happy to have her daily talks with The Analyst.

"He's not so bad, I suppose," Mother started.
Da' rarely got this opportunity, "I told you so."
She smirked at him.

Recognition

"He's quite bright you know; he has a good head on his shoulders that one," she went on.

"Oh, does he now?" Da' said in a mocking tone.

"Do you think our daughter would have settled for anything less than brilliant?" he added.

Mother smiled.

Though the winter was particularly harsh, none of them seemed to notice.

They were content in their new wee family life.

Spring approached, and they were all pleased to get outside and enjoy the sun and air. This particular evening, he asked Da' to join him in a walk along the loch, and she stayed with her mother in the garden near the house.

The rest of the evening was the same. Supper, and then off to engage in long talks as couples.

Mother and Da' went to the sitting room.

"So?" Mother asked.

"He asked for her hand in marriage."

"I knew it!" Mother shouted.

"How did you know?" Da' asked.

"I just knew it!" she said.

"You know everything," he mused.

She nodded in agreement.

"So, what did you say?" Mother asked.

"Oh, I thought you knew that as well," Da' teased.

She narrowed her eyes.

"Of course, I said yes."

"Good."

"Oh, good, is it? You've changed your tune," Da said.

She smiled.

"Does he know when he'll ask her?" she questioned Da'

"He didn't say, I'm sure he'll wait for the right moment."

She nodded.

Da' got up from his chair.

"Where are you going?" she asked.

"To check on the two of them."

"Leave them be," she directed.

"Leave them be!? You have been sending me up there every evening like the bloody Night Watchman to check on them, and now I can leave them be?" he asked.

She waved her hand at him dismissively.

He sat back down.

"You drive me mad, woman!"

She laughed.

The Wedding Day:

She wore a white dress. White wedding dresses became very popular after the Queen wore white at her wedding. Mother insisted. It had to be white.

The weather was cooperating beautifully. It was a gorgeous day in May. They chose to conduct the ceremony at their favorite spot overlooking the loch, on the top of the hill where they first met.

Mother and Cook prepared a feast for the wedding party and guests.

The couple arranged a honeymoon getaway to the Isle of Skye. They would leave the following morning to begin their lives together.

Da', after walking down the aisle with his daughter, took her hand and offered it to the Country Analyst. She belonged to him now, and he belonged to her.

Da' took his seat next to Mother.

Mother began, "isn't she beautiful?"

"Just like you when we got married," Da' said.

Mother blushed and playfully hit his arm, "that was a million years ago."

"Two million," Da' teased.

They laughed.

Mother reminded him of the story he told her when the kids first met. When he observed the couple at the market. Two flames, burning bright, strong, in unison.

"You were right, they are two flames," she said to Da'.

He reveled in hearing he was right.

Recognition

"Two flames, ignited by one spark," she went on, "it is as if they've known each other for centuries. Soulmates."

Da' nodded.

"She will see him at his worst, and she'll still think he's the best" Da' said, "she loves him so completely."

Mother nodded.

"It is the same for him," she added, "he looks at her like she's the very air he breathes; she is his life, a part of him."

They quieted now to listen to the couple exchange their vows…

Mother began to cry.

Da' took her hand and gave it a squeeze.

The couple kissed; pronounced man and wife.

Five
The United States of America
2022

She sat thinking about her past relationships and interactions with men. It had always felt as though she was fighting against them rather than loving them. Defending herself against their aggressions, their snide comments, or their hurtful actions. Love never seemed to come into it.

She was confident, independent, fiery, and strong. This was appealing for only so long.

Eventually, her traits became a problem for some of the men in her life. It wouldn't be long before their weakness and her strength would mix like water and oil.

They always seemed to try to break her down. They would ridicule her strength and confidence, speak down to her, and belittle her at any opportunity. There weren't many physical

Recognition

altercations, but on the rare occasions it got physical, they'd often try to overpower her.

Unsuccessfully.

This wasn't all men. There were men in her life that could match her, strength for strength. But these men would often become close friends of hers, not romantic partners.

Her dating pool, unfortunately, was plentiful in weakness and insecurity.

And so, her love life was nonexistent.

However, she thrived in solitude. Unlike most people, she was genuinely happy on her own.

In most situations she would choose solitude over coupling.

She never felt lonely in life.

Being lonely was not the worst feeling in life; it was being forgotten. Especially if you had cared deeply for the person who had forgotten you.

She had spent many years avoiding men and romantic relationships.

She liked her space, and she didn't want to answer to anyone.

And then, she met him, and something had changed. He wasn't like the rest, or so she thought.

He was the first person in years to hold her interest. She liked him instantly in a way she had rarely experienced in the past. And for an incredibly brief moment, there was a glimmer of hope.

Hope can often be concerning for The Singleton. Singleton's have essentially lived their lives alone. As in her case, she was utterly alone in life. She had great friends, but her family had since passed, she had no partner, and it was just her left in the world. Always <u>just</u> her. Finding the glimmer of hope when you think you've found a suitable partner can be very scary. It launches you into the unknown. She knows solitude, she doesn't know how to couple.

When she first met him, as mentioned, she felt love for him. Though more specifically, he was someone she wanted in her life for the long haul. Whether that meant a long-term friendship or something more, it didn't matter. He was someone she had hoped would stay in her life indefinitely.

Recognition

She had previously felt this way for people in her life, though it was very few and far between. In those instances, those people became very close friends, family.

She always believed the real staying power was in friendship. Romance, sex, even love could fade in time.

Even the couples she thought would last forever were now filing for divorce after 25 or 30 years of marriage. Things change.

Friendship lasted.

One of her ex-boyfriends called to see how she was doing. He was one of the good ones, and they remained friends throughout. A breakup didn't ruin them but improved their relationship. Better off as friends.

"So, how is everything going?" he asked.

"I'm good. You know, same old."

"Any men in your life?"

"Why is that always your first question? Not everything in life is about having a man!"

"Just wondering."

"I thought there was someone, but he ghosted me."

"What!? That's impossible. No one would ghost you. Are you sure he's not dead? Did you check the obituaries?"

She laughed, not at the thought of his possible demise, she never wished him any harm, quite the opposite in fact. But her ex's reaction was kindly meant and complimentary.

"He's fine," she said, not exactly sure if that was true.

"I feel bad for the guy," he sympathized.

"Oh, I'm not going to lash out or anything!" She thought he was referring to her temper and her special knack for putting people in their place – swiftly.

"No, I know you won't go off on him or cause a scene. I just mean he has no idea what he is missing. You are an amazing friend to me, and to all the people in your life. You love us unconditionally. You've been there for me at times I know I did not deserve, but you never let me down. We have gone months or years without speaking, and when I find you again, you welcome me with open arms, no questions, no judgement."

"I totally judge you," she interjected, teasingly.

Recognition

He laughed, "well, all I know is, there were times in my life where you were the only one I could count on. He is seriously going to be missing out. And for those of us who were lucky enough to get to know you intimately… I know he is missing the opportunity of a lifetime."

"Stop flirting!" she directed. It was very sweet of him to say such lovely sentiments.

She changed the subject and asked him about his life, and his day-to-day goings on.

After her phone conversation was finished, she thought of him again, her Ghost. He seemed incredibly eager to get to know her during their brief encounter. He was questioning her about her life at a dizzying pace during those long late-night talks.

Perhaps he knew of an approaching deadline she knew nothing about.

At times, she felt like a case study he was researching for some project. Trying to understand the way she lived her life, to incorporate it into his own, perhaps.

Elissa Ivy Siegel

Although the questions felt manic on occasion, it was still wonderful to meet someone who wanted to know her, truly. To understand her. The men she had been with in the past only wanted to talk about one thing. Themselves. They never really took the time to find out who she was as a person. He was different. He wanted to know her, and what's more, he listened to her. A captive audience, for a time anyway. She appreciated that more than he would ever know.

He was a little more closed off than she was; she could be an open book at times. But he was more reserved in sharing the parts of him that made him, him. But in the comfort and safety of their exchanges he started to share more of himself. She was very matter of fact, and straightforward. A real 'tell it like it is' type. He was more thought provoking and intentional about the things he shared, often leaving her to read between lines, to see deeper into the details he offered. Though she thought she saw him clearly, even when he was being vague. She never wanted to push him to share more, she foolishly thought they had time. 'He will open up more

Recognition

as we get to know each other better,' she had assumed. But they never got the chance for 'more'.

People were often fascinated by her life. She wasn't sure why. He seemed excited to learn all about it. She did what she wanted when she wanted. Fostering a somewhat hedonistic approach to life. Never thinking of it as impressive. It was just her way.

When she learned of his life and his accomplishments, she felt somewhat foolish. She said to him one evening, "ok, you've done some massively brilliant things in your life, and you're impressed by all the things I've done!? I've basically just done a bunch of stupid shit in my time," she laughed.

In truth, she was accomplished.

She would get an idea in her head, something she wanted to do, and she'd just go for it.

Her life was a bucket list, and much of it was already checked off.

Elissa Ivy Siegel

She could feel just as comfortable spending the weekend camping with friends as attending an international event with dignitaries on the guest list. And she didn't change her personality one bit between the two groups, or for everyone in between. They took her as she was.

She had an advanced degree, and she worked hard, but this didn't define her. She would rather focus on her experiences, and the people in her life. Work was a means to an end for her, she worked to travel, to experience life. Although she enjoyed her work, it was not where her ambitions lay.

So, in his study of her, maybe he would take a page from her book, and live life more fully.

Live freely, be bold, have fun.

As she told him during one of their all-night talks, "I don't like saying, 'life is short', that sounds terminal. But life is precious, and we must grab our opportunities, and chances where and when we can," she added, "if you want to do

Recognition

something, do it. Don't put it off for another day, grab the chance with urgency. Another day may never come."

Even though he hurt her with his silence, with this act of ghosting, she still wished him well. And she truly hoped that he was living his best life, whatever that might be.
Even if it was a life lived without her.

Six

Boston

1775

At night lying in the tent with the other boys, she would reach her hand out to hold onto him. He'd usually be asleep. She needed something, someone to hold onto. Other nights, when he was awake, he would take her hand in his, and they'd fall asleep like this.

As they grew closer in time, she wished she could do more than just reach out a hand. She longed for more than a touch. But that would betray who she really was to the other boys in the unit. A girl.

They met in December of '73 during the protest against the Tea Act.

In the chaos, she grabbed an apple from a food cart and legged it down the road, away from the crowds. He jumped her, knocking her to the ground. She wasn't ready for it. She

Recognition

hadn't seen him coming. Lying there the anger welled up in her face - crimson. He was shouting and reprimanding her for stealing the apple. He pulled her to her feet, and her cap fell off. Her long blonde hair flowed from the cap in waves down her back. He stood back and looked at her. "You're a GIRL!"

'He's not the brightest apple in the bunch, is he?' she thought.

"Why did you steal that apple?"

"Because I was hungry," She thought that was obvious. Is he dim?

"Why are you dressed like a boy?"

Ah, she supposed that was a valid question. And a much longer story.

He looked at her, expecting an explanation.

And so, she began.

As she spoke, he listened to her intently. She hadn't spoken this much in ages. It was nice to have someone to talk to, even nicer to have someone who listened. He watched her every move, taking in every word.

It was the usual sad story, she supposed.

Elissa Ivy Siegel

Her parents had died. She didn't have any other family in town. She was an orphan, alone on the streets. In the months after their deaths, she quickly realized it wasn't safe for a young girl on the streets alone. So, she became a boy. Growing up she was always the strongest of all her friends, the boys included. They would say, "you're really strong for a girl." She would say, "I'm really strong, full stop!" Underneath her clothes she wrapped the more feminine contours of her developing body, tucked her hair securely under her cap, and off she went. A boy.

With the rising tensions she wanted to do something to help the fight. She knew there was a group of boys helping with the efforts against the British. The Boston Boys, she heard they were called. So, she joined them. They'd run messages for the generals and commanders and complete other errands as needed. She was good at it. At one time in her life, she would walk into a room, and everyone would notice. Now she had learned to be invisible.

Head down, nose clean. Job done.

Well, invisible until today. How did he see her take that apple!? She was careful not to be seen.

He looked at her in disbelief. "You're a Boston Boy?".

She rolled her eyes. People always underestimated her. Though she knew how to use that to her advantage.

"Yes, I am!"

She learned that he was also working with The Boys, and they were equally surprised they hadn't run into each other before now.

She looked at him now with big soulful eyes, turning on a bit of that feminine charm she hadn't used in quite a long while, and asked him to keep her secret.

"Please don't tell them who I am. I'm not sure what the repercussions would be if I'm found out, but I do know I'd be put back on the streets at the very least."

He looked at her, deciding what to do. That look felt like an eternity.

She was going through the scenarios in her head while he thought it through. She assumed he'd rat her out. He was all bent out of shape over an apple. Bloody law-abiding citizen!

She didn't blame him. It wasn't his responsibility to keep her secret. Perhaps she was asking too much of him.

She started to back away and turned to go.

"Where are you going!?"

"Unless you're going to arrest me for stealing an apple, I'd rather have a head start out of here, while you tell the boys who I really am."

"I'm not going to tell them."

In this moment, she thought his face looked familiar, and quite pleasing. A feeling came over her that she quickly suppressed. Pushed aside. Maybe he was just familiar because they had seen each other in the streets these last weeks, months. She wasn't sure.

"Thank you."

He suggested they stick together. He proposed she come back to his unit with him.

Until now, she had been on her own. She was one of The Boys, yes, but she moved about independently, helping wherever she could, and ultimately remaining unseen. She wasn't sure she should accept his offer to stay together. But she followed him anyway.

In the months and year or so to follow, they found that they worked very well together. Everyone else realized it too. They quickly became the favorite duo, selected by the generals for more extensive operations. Dispersed together throughout the city and surrounding areas. Some of the work was top secret. They couldn't talk about it with the other boys. The boys never questioned them, but they often distanced themselves from the duo. They were the chosen ones. Or rather, he was the chosen one. But since they were inseparable, everyone unofficially treated them like a package deal. Partners.

Where he went, she went. And vice versa. Their strengths complemented each other.

He was intelligent, cunning, and had a charm that took everyone in. Everyone liked him immediately. He was fit, strong, and fast. All of which was helpful in creating a soldier. His brilliance seemed to have no bounds; he wasn't as dim as she had originally thought, she would often say to him teasingly. Everyone knew The General from Virginia was grooming him for something more. And she was along for the ride.

She had her strengths as well, of course.

Having mastered the art of invisibility, she could sneak in and out of the most challenging of high security areas, often while he was turning on the charm and distracting the guards. Although she was big for a girl, she was small for a boy. And once again, underestimated. She looked small, weak, unthreatening. Though she was anything but.

She wasn't only strong; she knew how to fight. She fought hard, with a fiery aggression, and methodic approach to cause maximum damage. Often the intense look on her face alone would diffuse the situation, and the fight would never come to pass.

All the boys said they felt safe around him (her).

They knew he (she) would fight to the death for them.

And she would. Especially for him.

Recognition

They spent their days walking all around the city, and from town to town running documents here and sourcing information there. They woke early each morning. Her hand clasped in his upon waking.

Why did they hold hands, she wondered?

It wasn't romantic, surely.

They were friends, partners in arms, trusted allies, Patriots. Though from her perspective, he was family. Her only family.

It's the summer of '74. They chatted nonstop as they walked through Cambridge on the way to their next appointment. It should be an easy one today. A quick grab and snatch. As always, he reminded her that if they got split up then they should meet at their special spot – the apple cart on the pier. Where it all began.

Did it begin there, she thought?

He was going on and on. His brilliance often resulted in a lot of chattiness. She didn't mind. She liked listening to him, for the most part.

"I hate the Redcoats." He was saying. "I can't stand the British!"

She didn't say anything.

She was thinking of the mission at hand. Even though it was a straightforward task today, she still liked to go over every eventuality in her mind. 'What do I do if this happens?', 'if we get captured, what plan is in place for an escape?', 'what if we get split up and he's not at the apple cart?'…

Once she was convinced that she had a plan in place for every occurrence, she came back to the conversation.

She hadn't realized he had stopped talking. He was looking at her. Staring most ardently.

It made her feel exposed. Known. Seen.

"WHAT ARE YOU STARING AT!?" she asked, as she punched him in the shoulder.

It seemed to break him from a trance, and he laughed.

"Nothing." (Everything)

Recognition

They walked on, and soon their destination was before them. They split up and started to implement the plan they put in place. He distracts, she grabs.

From her position at the back of the building she could hear him speaking to the guard.

Idle chit chat. 'Guy talk' as she called it. She smiled. Everyone liked him, even the enemy. With a shake of her head, she entered the building and made her way to the offices at the top of the stairs.

This was supposed to be easy, but not this easy. She didn't have to worry about being seen. No one was around. Where was everyone!?

She grabbed the maps and left the way she got in. The maps stashed securely in the wrapping she uses to diminish her curves. She stepped back on the street. Mission accomplished.

Then she heard the commotion. She peered around the corner. The guard had him on his back, several of them stood over him, hitting him repeatedly with heavy clubs and sticks.

A look came over her face. The look that silences men and makes them tremble.

She charged into the riot, head on. She'd have to be quick, there were too many of them.

Hit hard, make it count.

They didn't see her approach. She plowed her knee firmly into the crotch of the guard who stood over him. The guard doubled over. As she turned to kick the second guard at the outer side of his knee, busting his kneecap, she could see her companion getting to his feet.

At least we were two.

He handled the other two, while she landed a strong uppercut to the third guards' nose, splattering blood all over the street.

She grabbed her partner by the shoulder, and they started running.

He was faster than she was, much faster. But he never left her side.

Recognition

In that moment she wondered if she was actually holding him back. The thought was pushed aside.

"We should split up," she said.

He nodded and took off running ahead. He was faster than she remembered.

She ducked into an alley way, jumped a fence, and headed for the riverbank.

Two guards followed her. Three followed him.

She thought about the maps. The two of them had set up 'drop stations' all around the city and surrounding towns months ago. So far as they could tell, they were the only two to know about those locations. It helped in situations like these. Never get caught with the evidence. Additionally, her next move was to jump in the river, and the maps wouldn't survive the water.

With the maps safely in one of their drop stations. She slipped into the water quietly, trying not to make a splash. She floated close to the bank, hoping to slip out of view quietly.

She was a very good swimmer. He could outrun her any day, but in the water she was champion. His muscle mass made him sink. He could swim well enough, but it took double the effort to stay afloat. She always won when they would race in swimming.

When they were relieved from duties, they would often escape to a secluded pond they were sure few people knew about - a place where she could go and be a girl again. Removing the wrapping and taking her hair down, she would slip into the water and swim away, leaving him watching her from the shore.

He'd always wait on the shore, waiting for her to invite him in. As if he wanted to give her a moment to be herself. A moment to let her hair down, to free her ever growing curves from their shackles, to swim and feel a small amount of freedom.

It wouldn't be long before she would turn around and summon him into the water.

She'd always yell something like "come on scaredy cat, jump in! If you sink, I'll save you."

Recognition

He'd always smile.

She loved those summer days.

As she floated down the river, letting the Dirty Water carry her away to a safer location, she thought of him. What was her plan again if he wasn't at the apple cart?

He wasn't at the apple cart.

Sometimes, when someone disappears, she thought, there wasn't much you could do about it but wait.

In the last few days, or weeks rather, she did all she could do to find him.

She waited at that apple cart for days. Searching the pier, and the surrounding area. She had to wait there just in case he came back.

She reached out to The Boys, putting the word out that he had gone.

She even approached The General to tell him of their altercation with the guards while retrieving the maps. She removed the maps from their drop station and handed them to The General. All he could say was "I'm sure he'll be just fine." It wasn't comforting.

After searching the camps and sick bays, she made her way to the place where they brought the bodies. It took everything she had to go there. He couldn't be there, he wasn't dead. She looked over the corpses that were about his size. One matched his build, same hair color. The poor boys' face was so badly beaten she couldn't tell if it was him. Then she saw his ear. Relief. "It's not him," she said to the caretaker.

"How to you know this boy is not your friend?" the caretaker asked.

"My friend has a scar on his ear. You can see here; this boy has no such scar."

The caretaker nodded.

"I will be sure to keep an eye out for anyone matching his description, and I will contact you if there is any news," he spoke, "though, I hope never to have to share such news," he added.

Recognition

He was very kind. She thought about how incredible it was to deal with so much death each day, and yet remain so kind in this world. It took great courage.

As the weeks turned into months, she was desperate to find him.

She had one last option left. She rummaged through her old belongings. The things that were left untouched for some time. After removing some items of clothing and several documents, she made her way across town.

She would have to let her hair down for this one.

Infiltrating the British camps and meeting houses was her specialty after all, this was the only place she hadn't searched for him, until now. It was time to step back into her old life. It wasn't easy for her, she had become very comfortable, being a boy. It was safe.

The dress barely fit her; she was becoming quite the young lady. The wraps wouldn't hold her curves for much longer, she thought. With her documents in her handbag, she could freely walk around British territory. People didn't question her, a lovely young lady out for a stroll, unthreatening.

She searched the territory for much of the day. There was no sign of him.

Defeated, she walked to the pond where they spent most of their summer days together.

She stood at the shoreline looking out over the water. She stood there for quite some time, trying to think of her next steps. What more could she possibly do to find him?

A rustle in the tree line shook her from her thoughts. It was a Redcoat. Just what she bloody needed, she thought, trying to gather some patience for this encounter. She tried to muster up a smile and offered a forced pleasantry.

"What is a nice young lady like you doing out here all by yourself?" he asked.

"Just taking the air," she offered.

He stepped closer to her, too close.

She looked up at him, her smile faded, and her eyes narrowed. The nature of men. She could see it coming a mile away.

Recognition

He reached out and put his hand around her waist, pulling her in.

She steadied herself, her hands on his chest, struggling to push him away.

She tried to be polite. If this ended in a confrontation, she would be the one to blame.

"Please sir, as you say, I am a nice young lady; please mind your manners," she pleaded.

"All I want is a little kiss, surely you wouldn't begrudge a soldier a kiss?"

(She'd sooner kick this soldier in his teeth than kiss him.)

"But I am spoken for (a lie), my gentleman friend would not approve," she was trying her best not to clock him in the teeth.

He leaned in and kissed her, ignoring her protest.

He pulled her in, he was strong. She was locked in his grip. This one wasn't going to be easy to fend off.

Her heart started to race, she wasn't scared exactly, she knew how to defend herself, but it could result in trouble. Trouble for her. Additionally, she could never know how a man would react in these situations. Most of them backed off when she used force, some of them fell in love with her (men!), and some of them fought back.

Just as she was about to do something very unladylike, a man came racing out of the woods and knocked the soldier to the ground. He had such a tight grip on her that she fell with them both.

She loosened his grip on her and freed herself from the altercation.

When she got to her feet, she saw him. It was her companion, her friend, her fellow Patriot. Found.

The two men fought for some time, before the soldier stood up. Spitting blood, he cursed them both, and made a comment about her "not being worth it". He walked off back towards the camps.

They stood for a moment in silence, staring at each other. Then she threw her arms around his neck and pulled him in for a hug.

"I leave you for a moment and while I'm gone you end up kissing a damned Redcoat," he teased.

Recognition

She punched him in the shoulder, laughing.

"You were gone for more than a moment," she spoke. "What happened to you!?"

"I was on orders from The General," he informed her.

Her eyes narrowed now. That look she gets when she has been betrayed. It's chilling. She rarely used it on him. She rarely had cause to.

His smile faded, and he felt the chill go through him. She was mad. He braced himself.

"Why the hell didn't you tell me?" she started. "I was worried about you. I have been searching for you for months. I TOUGHT YOU WERE DEAD!"

"I wasn't allowed to tell anyone. It was top secret."

Her face was growing ever more crimson.

"I am not just anyone," she spat.

"And The General was no help, all he could say was, 'he'll be fine,'" she added.

"I am fine," he offered.

In that moment she could have killed them both, him and The General. Well, if not kill them, inflict some pain at the very least.

"UGH!" she walked away.

He never offered any apology.

She didn't speak to him for quite some time.

Although she understood, she still felt betrayed. She understood that he couldn't say anything about the mission, but he could have let her know he was alright. Let her know he wasn't lying in a ditch somewhere. She didn't need the details of his assignment, but some common courtesy would have been nice. She had spent months searching for him, worrying for him, and now she was tired. She didn't have the strength to fight with him, so she remained silent.

The silence lasted for a very long time.

Recognition

Seven
The United States
2022

Singletons have very high standards. They have certain rules in place when it comes to the world of dating. People often mistakenly believe the opposite is true, they think singletons are desperate, up for anything, open to any sort of attention, or advance. This could not be further from the truth. Little do people realize, the singleton life is a choice. Though, every once in a while, they meet that one person who makes them want to break the rules.

After he left, she found herself breaking her own rules when it came to men or dating. Breaking these rules really pissed her off, but she did it anyway. She wasn't sure why. Their encounter was so brief, so why, with what was seemingly so little between them, could she not let go?

She wasn't giving up.

Recognition

This angered her. What the hell was so special about him!? She knew the answer.

But she also knew he had hurt her, and he was not worth her time and energy.

And yet, she gave it anyway.

She wasn't excessive in her correspondence, though that's subjective.

When he first left, she tried reaching out with a few light text messages, no more than three, spanning the course of the first month. A few messages to see how he was doing. Then she wrote a more long-winded email at the end of that month.

Perhaps that was a bit much.

She was often a bit much. She knew it.

The communications were just a friendly gesture, to ultimately say that the lines of communication were still open, at least on her end.

There was another reason behind her correspondence. And possibly why it was a little harder to let go. Before he left, he expressed some life stresses he was dealing with, and on the off chance that this silence was a result of that stress, she wanted to let him know she was still there if he needed anything.

He didn't deserve it, but she offered it anyway. If he needed anything, he could contact her.

All her correspondence was met with silence. Though if she was honest, she didn't want to hear from him. She hoped he would not respond.

What could she possibly say? What could he say?

His silence eventually became comforting. Like telling your secrets to a wall you know will never talk back.

She knew full well sending these messages made her look pathetic, foolish.

Recognition

She didn't care. She wasn't concerned with how she looked. She had the courage to be vulnerable. When she wanted to do something, she did it. She stood by her convictions.

The hope was that these messages were not causing him any irritation, or grief. She hoped they were received in the manner in which they were given, in friendship.

One final reason for sending these messages and hanging on as she had; there was a strong possibility that they may have to see each other in future social settings. So, even if he didn't want to speak to her, even if he didn't want her friendship, at the very least, he was going to have to take his head out of his ass and show some civility at some point. And she hoped the correspondence would ease the awkwardness of that meeting in some way. If that was even remotely possible.

And so, in hanging on as long as she had, and sending him these messages, she had broken all of her rules. She didn't let go of things easily, that was true, but this time it felt particularly difficult to let go. Which was strange because their encounter was 'nothing'.

Though it felt like something.

Recognition

Elissa Ivy Siegel

Eight

England

1953

(In a village just outside of Cambridge)

"Oi, Gramps! Are you listening to me?" she shouted.

The other ladies in the shop were looking on in shock.

Her son wasn't surprised, or embarrassed one bit. He was used to seeing his mother tell people off. It was a common occurrence.

This time she was yelling at the butcher for selling her a terrible cut of meat.

She never let anything slide. Never let it go. She always spoke up for herself, for him, for everyone in her life. She would go to battle for all of them. Even the small battles like this one.

Recognition

"Gramps!"

The butcher was not pleased with his new nickname.

"You expect me to feed this meat to my son? We got home, opened the wrapper, and it was all gristle and fat underneath."

"That there is a prime cut of meat," the butcher argued.

Her son started to shake his head; the butcher was a fool for arguing with her.

"A PRIME cut of meat!? Are you mad!?" she spat.

She turned to the other ladies in the shop and started getting them involved. At first, they hesitated to join in, but one spoke up, "yes, I got a bad cut of meat last week; my husband couldn't stomach it, we ended up throwing it out."

The other ladies started to join in, one after the other. Soon the butcher felt like he was about to have a riot on his hands.

"Ok, ok, ladies, please calm down."

No one should ever tell her to calm down.

"CALM DOWN? CALM DOWN? We will calm down when you give us good cuts of meat, at no cost, to make up for this crap you're trying to pedal!" she yelled.

The ladies chimed in, in unison. They backed her up.

The butcher complied, begrudgingly.

She got her cuts of meat and walked out, her son following behind.

"Come on Love Bug," she called behind her.

"Mum, I'm too old to be called your Love Bug any longer," he protested.

"I'll be calling you my Love Bug even when you're 30."

Lovebug

(The lovebug, also known as the honeymoon fly or double-headed bug, is a species of march fly. During and after

Recognition

mating matured pairs remain together, even in flight, for up to several days.)

Nan was coming for dinner and staying the weekend. After dinner, when Nan and her Love Bug were settling in for the night, she went back to the butcher shop.

He was just about to close up for the night.

He looked defeated and seeing her didn't improve his mood.

She held out a wad of cash.

"What is this?" he asked.

"It's not an apology. You were still wrong for selling poor quality meat. But I didn't intend to make such a scene and incur such a large expense by having you reimburse all the ladies in the shop. I guess I got a little carried away."

"A little?" he asked.

"Don't push it, Gramps."

He silenced himself.

"Look, I know I get fiery at times. But my son and I are on our own, and when I think we've been wronged, or treated poorly, I react," she explained.

He listened.

"But I didn't mean for it to cost you a full days' pay in meat costs," she went on. "So please, take the money."

His face softened. He reminded her of her father, they would have been about the same age, if her dad had lived.

"I can't take your money," he spoke. "You and your son are on your own, it wouldn't be right."

"Please take it. Before I lost my husband in the war he provided very well for his son and I," she confessed.

"Please," she added, handing him the cash again.

He took the money.

Recognition

"I lost my wife in the war as well. I'm sorry to hear about your husband," he consoled.

They were silent for a moment.

She still felt a little strange calling him her husband. But she complied with his wishes all these years. She acted as his widow, for her son.

"You should join us for dinner tomorrow night."

"Oh, I couldn't," he said.

"Yes, we won't take no for an answer. My friend Nan is staying with us, and she would love to meet you. My son told her all about the encounter at the shop today. I think she would feel better if she could see that you are alive and well after my attack this afternoon," she joked.

The Butcher laughed. He rarely did that these days.

He accepted her invitation.

(For the record, he never sold another poor cut of meat again.)

The Butcher comes to dinner:

Love Bug ran to the door to greet The Butcher, "Hello Gramps!" he said, so innocently, and so friendly, that it made the butcher laugh.

From then on, they always referred to him as Gramps. Another nickname that stuck.

The Butcher brought her son a bag of candy from the sweet shop.

Her son, wide-eyed, started to dive into the bag.

"LOVE BUG! Not until after dinner," she yelled from the kitchen.

"How did she know?" her son asked, looking at the butcher.

"Mothers always know," he replied.

Recognition

Love Bug nodded.

Everyone had a wonderful time at dinner.

They learned that the butcher was a contractor in his earlier years. A true handyman, working with carpentry, plumbing, electrical, and mechanical work. Now he just did odd jobs for friends or neighbors but building and engineering things was his passion. Her son thought this was fascinating, he had several questions for him.

"Gramps, can you make this?"

"Gramps, can you fix this?"

"Gramps, can you teach me how to build things?" and on and on.

The Butcher seemed delighted to answer all of Love Bug's questions.

He and his wife never had any children. He was enjoying every bit of his conversation with her son.

After dinner, as she and Nan were cleaning up in the kitchen, the butcher and her son went into the parlor.

"You know, I didn't think I liked your mum at first," The Butcher started.

He added, "she is quite scary, but when you get to know her, she's actually a very kind, very fair person."

"People often misunderstand her in the beginning," her son offered. "But in the end, they realize that she's a good person to have in their corner."

The Butcher agreed, "she's definitely someone you want on your side!"

"She doesn't take any shit from anyone," Love Bug said matter-of-factly.

The butcher looked surprised, and then laughed a hearty laugh.

"It's ok, mum lets me curse at home. She curses like a sailor and has always said that she can't very well tell me not to do it when she uses such language. I am not allowed to curse at school or in public though, I must be polite," he explained.

The Butcher smiled.

In the kitchen, she was teasing Nan about The Butcher. She could swear she sensed something between them.

"Don't go playing matchmaker now," Nan insisted.

"I'm just saying, I think he showed some interest in you. And you seemed interested in return, that's all."

Nan didn't say anything.

"I thought I saw a spark between you," she added.

"A spark!? At our age?" Nan questioned.

"Sparks have no time limit," she was sure.

Nan smiled.

The ladies moved to the parlor and sat down to have a drink with The Butcher. After a few sips she excused herself and Love Bug.

"It's time for someone to go to bed." She said, standing up and walking towards her son.

He gave a little protest, but then he saw the look on her face and complied.

They said their good nights, and she invited The Butcher and Nan to stay and talk for as long as they'd like, she was off to bed herself.

Nan looked at her suspiciously. 'She's matchmaking,' Nan thought.

Upstairs she was trying to settle him into bed. She was stroking his dark hair and listening to him chatter on and on

Recognition

about their night. About Gramps. About Nan. About Nan and Gramps.

He could see what she saw.

"I think Nan and Gramps like each other," he concluded.

She smiled, "I think so too."

"Is that why we had to go to bed early?"

"You know me too well."

He grinned.

"Tell me about the time you met Daddy," he requested.

"Again!"

"Yes, again!"

Her son had always loved this story. It wasn't a long story, but Love Bug always marveled at the idea that they very nearly didn't meet at all. It was completely by chance. And her son liked to say it was a miracle that they had met.

"Well, it was just before the war began. My best friend wanted me to join her at a dance they were having in town. One of the boys she liked would be there, and she tried to drag me along. But I said, 'NO'. I had worked all day. I was dead on my feet, and I was adamant that I was NOT going with her," she started.

Love Bug smiled. He knew this story by heart.

"In one last attempt to get me to go, she stopped by my house on the way to the dance. But I was still firm, the answer was NO."

"You know how I get when I don't want to do something," she said to Love Bug.

He nodded in understanding.

"So, shortly after my friend left for the dance, I noticed that she left her handbag behind. I couldn't very well let her go without her purse, so I headed to the dance to give it to her," she explained (for the millionth time.)

Recognition

"I ran out of the house without so much as tidying my hair. I was wearing trousers, which was not the fashion at the time for a dance, and I barely had any make-up on. I was a vision!" she joked.

Love Bug laughed.

"Anyway, I was trying to get in and out of the dance very quickly. I just wanted to give her the purse, and get out of there, but in my haste, I slipped on the stairs, and nearly fell, headfirst."

"But Daddy caught you!" Love Bug blurted out.

"He did. He reached out and caught me before I could go tumbling down the stairs."

"You were the catch of the day!" her son mused.

She laughed, "Yes, I guess I was!"

"What happened next?" he asked.

"You know what happens next!" she teased him.

"Well, he didn't seem to notice what a mess I was, or how clumsy I was nearly falling down the stairs. He still had his arms around me to steady me from the fall when he asked me to dance. And I said…"

"And you said, 'well since I'm already in your arms, we might as well make our way to the dance floor'." Love Bug finished.

"See, you do know this story," she teased.

"And so, we danced and talked the whole night, and we took that photograph there that you have on your dresser. That's the two of us just outside the dance hall," She pointed to the photo across the room.

"And you fell in love from then on?" Love Bug asked.

"Yes, we did."

Her son was quiet for a moment, he was picturing the scene in his mind, their first meeting, and how it nearly didn't happen.

Recognition

Sometime later he asked, "Why do you love Daddy?"

For a woman who always had something to say, she found herself speechless.

No one had ever asked her that before. She never really gave it much thought.

She just loved him. She never thought about the 'why'.

He asked again, "what made you fall in love with him?"

She thought back to when they first met. She couldn't remember a time when she didn't love him. Was it love at first sight? It wasn't that exactly.

It was more a sense that they had always been in love. She wasn't sure how to explain it.

"Well, there are a lot of things I love about your father. He was kind, and intelligent, and very funny. He always made me laugh."

Her son smiled.

"And he never seemed to mind my fiery temper; he enjoyed it for the most part. He was very strong, not just physically, but he was strong in character, and he was very brave."

"Your father and I shared and respected each other's values and goals in life."

She thought about him for a moment.

"I suppose I truly loved him because I saw something in him that was, familiar. When I looked at him, it was as if we had known each other forever. As if, he was meant to be my person. We didn't have to speak to know what the other was thinking or feeling. We just knew one another. Completely."

Her son was taking this all in, thinking it over.

"You were soulmates," Love Bug concluded.

"Yes, I guess we were (are)."

"Now, get some sleep my love bug. I love you."

Recognition

"Good night Mumma, I love you too."

She felt a little drained. Sometimes thinking of him did that, it took everything out of her.

Other times she'd think of him and gain strength from it, like those times she could feel him near, a strength at her side.

But tonight, she was drained.

It's hard keeping someone alive in your memory. Someone you barely had a chance to know. It was as if they had known each other completely, but at the same time they were strangers.

From the start, she wanted to keep him alive for her son's sake. She wanted him to know his father. She had very few photographs of him, but the ones she did have, she made copies of and put them all around the house. She would tell her son stories of their brief time together. And she would try to answer Love Bug's ever-growing list of questions about his father. Even though she wasn't always sure she had the answers.

Was she building up the correct picture of him?

She went downstairs and found Nan in the kitchen; she was cleaning up the drinking glasses.

Nan looked at her and put the kettle on. "Let's have a chat."

They settled around the kitchen table.

"So, tell me about the butcher," She said to Nan.

"In a minute, first tell me why you look so drained," Nan instructed.

She smiled. Either her face was giving an obvious impression, or Nan knew her very well.

"It's nothing, I was telling Love Bug about his father again."

"And?"

Recognition

She shrugged, "I don't know, sometimes I think I didn't know him at all. It felt like we truly knew each other, but did we? We never had the time to learn more about one another."

Nan looked sad on her behalf.

She went on, "Love Bug has so many questions about him; it is natural for him to want to know his dad, but I don't always have the answers. At times, they are the simplest of questions."

A few months back he came home from school and asked, "What was dad's favorite color?"

"Green." She answered, though she wasn't quite sure if that was true.

The next day he arrived home from school with a picture he had drawn. It was of the three of them standing outside their house. His dad, wearing a green shirt, her, and Love Bug.

It pained her, he had drawn the life they could have had, filling in the parts of their lives that were missing. Lost. Him.

"In any case," she told Nan, "It's easy to idolize someone who's gone. I think many people do this, they put the dead on a pedestal. We were together for such a short time, he disappears, and it's easy to say, 'he was a hero', 'he would have been an amazing dad', 'a loving husband', etc. But who knows!?"

Nan looked shocked, "you don't think he would have been all of those things?"

"I do think he would have been all those things, but I also think that it wouldn't have been perfect. We wouldn't be playing happy families, in some fairytale story. Things, at times, would have been hard. There would have been fights, and hardships, and struggles. It may sound odd, but I miss not having those hardships with him. That would have been real."

"And now what do we have," she went on, "some romantic fairytale, of our short encounter."

Recognition

"I've made him into a bloody superhero with my stories to Love Bug but is it real?" she added.

Nan thought about it for a while.

"Your love for him was real. Your love gave you a son. That is real." Nan said.

She knew Nan was right, her heart ached.

Nan went on, "if he came back from the war, maybe it would have been all happy families, and wonderful, or maybe it wouldn't have worked out. We will never know. But for the brief time you were in each other's lives, it was real."

"Just tell Love Bug what you can about him, and the things you don't know, tell him you don't know," said Nan. "How much do we really know about anyone anyhow?" she concluded.

She nodded.

"So, tell me about the butcher." She insisted, with a smile.

"He's going to visit me in London next weekend to take a look at my pipes," said Nan, "we've had a leak in the kitchen sink at the house."

"Oh, is that what they're calling it these days? He's 'taking a look at your pipes'!?" she teased.

Nan hit her on the arm, "the things you say!"

"I didn't say anything, it was merely implied."

They both laughed.

Gramps became a permanent fixture in their lives. Love Bug would take to Gramps' garage most days after school, and on the weekends. Assuming Gramps wasn't visiting Nan in London on the weekends.

They'd spend hours in his garage fixing things, building this or that. Her son loved spending time with him. And Gramps couldn't be more pleased.

Recognition

She loved that her son was learning such skills. Love Bug was intelligent. Like his father, he was academically gifted, but she was happy he was learning this trade as well, to be handy, and truly skilled at this work he and Gramps were doing together. She was also pleased he had a man in his life that he could talk to, someone other than his mum and Nan.

As the months passed by, they started to become quite the close-knit family.

Her, Love Bug, Nan, and now Gramps.

This was the family they made along the way, not in blood, not on paper, but in feeling and love. Nan and Gramps felt like parents to her, and grandparents to him.

She was especially thankful for the latter.

She was standing on a stepstool, tidying the bookshelves in their house, when Love Bug came home from school.

Elissa Ivy Siegel

"Mumma?"

"Yes, darling," she said without turning around.

"Why don't I look like you?" he asked.

"You act like me, isn't that enough?" she teased.

He laughed.

"What's this all about?" she asked.

She turned and stepped down from the stool.

"A boy at school pointed out that we look nothing alike," He said, sitting on the sofa looking deflated.

She knelt in front of him and brushed his dark hair out of his eyes. (He needs a haircut, she thought.)

Taking his face in her hands, she said, "you look like your father, you know that."

"I know."

"Was this boy mean to you?" she asked.

Recognition

"No, he didn't mean any offense, he was just curious."

"Ok."

She looked at him for a while; he was mulling something over in his head.

"I think he wondered if I had a father. He assumed it was just the two of us," he started.

"Ah, I see."

"May I bring Daddy's picture with me to school tomorrow?" he asked.

"Of course, you may my love. Would you like the one of Daddy in his uniform, from the war?"

"No, I want the one of the two of you at the dance." (His favorite.)

"Ok, love. We will pack it with your school things tonight."

"Thanks Mum. Can I go visit Gramps now?"

"Yes, but I want you home for supper. You can invite Gramps to join us, but I want you both back here at 6:00pm on the dot!"

"Ok, ok."

"I mean it. If I have to come looking for you two in that garage, you'll be in big trouble. BIG TROUBLE mister!" she added.

Her son laughed.

She was threatening to everyone in the world, but not her son. He saw right through her.

She smiled, "tell Gramps I say hello."

He threw his arms around her neck and gave her a quick kiss as he raced out the door.

Recognition

The following day, she walked Love Bug to school. His teacher requested they meet this morning, though she didn't say what it was regarding.

Her son, who had the photo of his parents securely placed in his rucksack, happily ran off to join the other boys in the yard.

She entered the school to meet with his teacher.

After the meeting she walked to work. She was working part-time at the university.

As she walked along the river, she thought about their meeting.

"Your son is very intelligent; he is far beyond the rest of his class academically. We would recommend advancing him to a higher level," the teacher began.

"What would that entail?"

"Next year, he would start two levels above his current grade. This would mean he will be in a class with children who are two to three years his elder," the teacher explained.

"Are there other options, rather than advancing him a level? He is happy here with his friends, and classmates."

"You could get him a tutor. He could remain with his class, but eventually, he will outgrow them academically. In the meantime, the tutor will at least help him to develop his knowledge, and academic prowess."

"Thank you for letting me know our options. I will speak to my son tonight and we will decide together," She informed the teacher.

These were the times she wished his father were here. She had fears that by putting her son in a higher level with older kids, bigger kids, he would get bullied. She could only think of how big those other children looked. Was it an irrational fear? Was she holding him back, by hoping he would remain with his current class? His dad would have known what to do.

As she walked, she thought about something that happened a few months back. She was trying to help Love Bug with his math's. She hated math's. Another reason she wished his father was still with them. She was more of an English lit, history, psychology, kind of girl. She tested well enough in mathematics, so well in fact, that she didn't have to take the class again. It had been a long while since she had even looked at a math problem.

Now she was trying to help Love Bug with his work. Inadequately, she feared. They muddled through his course work that day and completed it, but she sensed her son was frustrated with her level of help. He went up to his room in a huff and slammed the door.

She stood there in an empty kitchen, and yelled into the air, "you left me to raise a genius on my own. AND I DON'T KNOW WHAT I'M DOING!"

She will speak to her son tonight, she thought. They could decide together, and whatever he chooses, she would support.

The Tutor:

Love Bug decided he would prefer to work with a tutor. They agreed that he would see the tutor for the remainder to the school year, and then they would decide if he felt ready to move up a level at school.

This felt like a good compromise, and she was happy he would be staying with his friends his own age for a while longer.

The school arranged the tutor for him. He was from the university. His focus was mathematics, science, and he had a knack for languages, much like her son. They proved to be a good match.

Recognition

The Tutor arrived at their house one afternoon for their first session.

She opened the door and greeted him. He was, what she would call, 'well made.'

She ignored the attraction and introduced him to her son.

The Tutor would work with her son three times a week, at their house, for the remainder of the school year.

At first, Love Bug was concerned he would miss out on his afternoons with Gramps, but she assured him he'd still have plenty of time with Gramps. And on the nights that the tutor was there, she would invite Gramps over for dinner, and the four of them, or the five of them, if Nan was visiting, would have dinner together. The Tutor lived on his own, so he welcomed the family dinners when he was invited. Though she only invited him when Gramps or Nan would be present. It didn't seem right somehow to have dinner, just the three of them.

Nan called one night, "so how's your boyfriend?" she teased.

"He's not my boyfriend! He is here to tutor Love Bug, nothing more."

"Ah, but you knew who I was talking about," Nan said.

She smiled, "he's doing well, but he's not my boyfriend."

"You've had a lot of male suitors over the years, and you're always pushing them away," Nan went on. "Give this one a chance."

"We'll see," she placated.

"I know what 'we'll see' means. It means 'no'. You can't keep comparing everyone to him. You had your one great love in life, and maybe there won't be another, but it doesn't mean that these men can't provide a certain companionship," Nan scolded.

She felt a flash of anger. She wasn't comparing everyone to him. Was she?

"I don't compare these men to him," she argued.

"Oh please, you say you've built him up as a superhero in your stories to Love Bug, but the truth is, you've built him up as a hero in your mind as well. He wasn't a bloody Saint!" Nan argued.

"Ok, ok, why are you so worked up about this?" she asked.

"I just love you and I want you to me happy. I worry that you're holding onto ghosts," Nan said.

"Ok, if the tutor asks me out, I will not say no. That's the best I can do right now," she offered.

"Ok." Nan was pleased.

A few weeks later, The Tutor asked her to join him for dinner.

He found her in her office at the University.

She looked up surprised, she wasn't aware he knew where her office was located.

He was standing in the doorway. He stood about 6 foot 2 inches tall, with a lean, muscular build, sandy blonde hair, blue eyes, and a chiseled jaw.

"Hi," she spoke, "do we need to talk about Love Bug's sessions?"

"No, I'm not here in a professional capacity. I just wanted to say 'hello'."

"Ah, ok, 'hello'," she said, starting to get annoyed. She hoped he would get to the point quickly; she was at work after all.

She looked at him, waiting.

"Can I take you to dinner tomorrow night?" he finally asked.

She paused for a moment.

"Why don't we have a nice picnic lunch on the green, by the river tomorrow instead?" she proposed.

"Yes, that sounds nice, shall I come by the house to pick you up." he asked.

Recognition

He was sweet she thought, the green wasn't very far from her house, she could walk and meet him by the river. But she thought about Nan and responded, "sure, you can come by the house."

He smiled.

"I'll plan everything, I'll make lunch and have everything prepared," he added.

"Ok, that sounds nice. I look forward to it."

"Me too." he said, smiling.

The following day was lovely.

He arrived at the house with a large picnic basket full of goodies.

He and Love Bug spoke in French for a little while, until it was time to head out.

Nan, and Love Bug waved them off from the doorway.

It was a beautiful, sunny, Saturday afternoon.

He packed an elaborate lunch, with treats and champagne.

"You made all of this?" she asked.

"Well, I actually had them prepare it for me at the Tea Room in the village," he admitted.

She laughed, "you know I could have just made us sandwiches."

"No, I wanted to do this for you," he offered.

"Thank you, it's lovely."

He smiled.

As he popped the chilled champagne, she dove into the sandwiches and grabbed a salmon and cucumber square.

"Mm, these are delicious! They do a good job at the Tea Room," she teased.

They finished lunch and the bottle of champagne, as they talked and laughed, passing the day away.

Recognition

Later they went punting on the river. This was one of her favorite pastimes. Cambridge looked so beautiful from the water.

After a few turns up and down the river, he moored the punt in a secluded, serene area.

They laid down together and looked up at the sky and the weeping willows.

He took her hand in his. They laid here for a while like this, in silence.

She took his arm and placed it around her, so that she could move in and rest her head on his chest. The movement of the boat was soothing. They were comfortable, content.

They held each other and spoke about their lives, about Love Bug, Nan, Gramps, about his family, about their pasts. The hours went by and before they knew it, it was supper time.

"Join us for supper tonight," she offered. "Gramps is coming over and we're going to have a special dinner and some birthday cake for Nan and Love Bug's birthdays."

"They have the same birthday?" he asked.

"Yes, it's tomorrow. He was born on her birthday, and they have been inseparable ever since," she smiled. "Love Bug is having his friends from school over for a little party tomorrow afternoon. You're welcome to come to that as well, if you're brave enough to take on a dozen youths running around the house."

He laughed, "I'll be there."

As she was tucking Love Bug into bed after his birthday party, he asked, "why do you call me Love Bug?"

"Uh-oh, did I slip up and call you Love Bug in front of your friends today?" she asked. (This was strictly forbidden.)

Recognition

"No, you didn't. I was just curious."

"Well, Nan used to call your dad and I love bugs. Connected. Attached. And when I was pregnant with you, you sort of felt like a little bug moving around in my belly, and I started calling you my little Love Bug" she explained.

He thought about it for a moment.

"Nan says I was made from love," he asked, "what does that mean?"

Here it comes, she thought, the sex talk.

He added, "how did you and daddy make me?"

She didn't need to explain the love they felt for each other, Love Bug knew all about that.

She taught him the science of it all; how men and women, and animals, all came together to create life. She explained the cycle of life. She explained the pleasure in being intimate with someone whom you liked or loved. She tried not to spare any details, in telling him the truth.

He listened carefully.

"Do you have to be in love to make the baby?" he asked.

"No, the baby is made in the science of it, not in the love," She replied, hoping she wasn't killing some romantic notion.

"Though, in your case, you were made in so much love, which is why Nan always says, 'you were made in love'" she added.

"So, you can still have sex, but not be in love?" he clarified.

"Yes."

"Do you love my tutor like you loved daddy?" he asked.

"No, not like I loved your father, but I do like him a lot," she confessed.

"Will you make more babies with him?" he inquired.

"No, I don't think so Love Bug."

"Ok."

He seemed content with that answer, she thought.

Recognition

"Do you have any other questions, my love?"

"No. I think I understand it now."

"Ok, Good Night, My Love Bug."

"Good night, Mumma, I love you."

"I love you more."

He smiled.

Elissa Ivy Siegel

Nine
The United States of America
(By way of Scotland)
2022

When it rains, it bloody pours.

She tossed her phone on the desk and walked out of the room. That was the seventh one to come out of the woodwork. Ex-boyfriends falling from the sky. It is nice that they are still in touch, she supposed, but she wasn't in the mood for this right now.

Typical of the universe, there was only one person she wanted to hear from, and instead, the past is haunting her.

On second thought, did she really want to hear from him? Her Ghost. If things had progressed with him, and then he pulled his disappearing act further into their relationship, it would have had the potential to really hurt her in the end. She had an annoying feeling that he was right. Though he went about it in the wrong way, he may have been right in pulling away as he did.

The more annoying feeling was that she knew it was wrong of her to hold on.

She hated it when she was wrong and someone else was right. It pissed her off to no end.

Maybe she had dodged a bullet, losing him sooner.

It was best he pulled out when he did.

Picking up her phone again, she turned off the notifications and hit the treadmill. Tune it all out.

There was someone she was talking to. Someone new.

The Scotsman.

She met The Scotsman on her last trip to the UK. They had met on the last day of her tour. She never expected to hear from him when she returned to the states, but he reached out, and things progressed from there.

The day she met him she didn't think she liked him very much. And yet, there was something about him. Something that stirred a reaction in her, though she thought the reaction was irritation.

Meeting The Scotsman:

She walked up to him and asked him a question.

He replied with a smart-ass remark that got her Irish up. A flash of anger crossed her face. It had already been a rough morning, and she wasn't in the mood for anyone's bullshit.

Her first thought was, 'I want to smack this guy; are we stuck with him for the entire day?' She was in a mood, but she tried to bite her tongue. It wasn't his fault she had had a tough morning.

The group got on the bus and headed into the Scottish Highlands for the day.

Recognition

She tried to settle into the ride, enjoy the scenery, and hopefully improve her mood. This was the last day of the trip, and she was not looking forward to leaving Scotland. She loved it there, drawn to the country. Additionally, there was a lot of shit going on at home that she wasn't eager to return to. Reality.

He was going on and on about something or other, she tried to tune him out.

This guy likes the sound of his own voice, she thought. Her mood wasn't improving.

The ride through the highlands was gorgeous. In time, she started to feel like herself, less irritated, and she was determined to enjoy her last day.

At the first stop on the tour, she stepped out to utterly amazing views. After taking a few photos, she walked back towards the bus. He was there. She stood next to him, waiting for the rest of the group to return. They engaged in idle chit-chat. She looked at him now, without so much aggression in her glance. He is attractive, I suppose, she thought. He gave her a look that made her feel... something.

A flash of heat ran through her, and she looked away.

After a time, she looked back. He was staring at her intently. Sizing her up. She suddenly felt tongue-tied, and what she would call 'all girly'. She felt irritated again, and she got back on the bus.

What the hell was that? she thought. Is he interested in me? She pushed the thought from her mind.

The tour bus took off to the next location.

Gazing out of the window, she thought about the look he gave her. There was a recognition between them. She thought he would be one of those men who could match her, strength for strength. This one could be trouble, she thought, the fun kind of trouble. She grinned.

Later at the next stop, he addressed the group with a slightly lascivious comment.

Recognition

Without hesitation, she tossed back a risqué retort in exchange.

The rest of the group didn't seem to understand their humor. They glanced at each other and smiled, before walking off in opposite directions.

For the remainder of the day, they seemed to be circling each other, a glance here, a witty comment there, neither one really making a move.

As the tour came to an end, some social media accounts were shared, and just like that, they were connected. Though, does that carry any weight in this day and age? We are all connected today.

(So much connection, and no one really knows anyone.)

A few weeks later, he contacted her.

Their conversations quickly went from catching up and getting to know each other, to something more sexual in nature.

He was fun and flirty. She enjoyed speaking with him.

He confessed that he wasn't sure if she was attracted to him when they met on the tour.

She smiled.

"You irritated me at first," she admitted, "but as the day went on, and with the looks we were exchanging, it made me think that I either wanted to kick you in the teeth or invite you to lift that kilt of yours and take me up against a wall in an alleyway somewhere."

(There's something about a man in a kilt.)

"Ha-ha. I much prefer the latter."

She laughed, "me too."

"I wasn't really sure if you were interested in me either," she added.

Recognition

"I was watching you most of the day. I liked the way you carried yourself," he confessed.

"How, overly confident, and a little bitchy?" she teased, remembering she was in a mood that day.

"Don't you mean overly bitchy, and a wee bit confident?" he teased.

This fucking guy, she thought, shaking her head, then she laughed, "yes, perhaps that was it."

She liked that he wasn't put off by her attitude the day of the tour. Strength for Strength.

He wasn't easily scared off, made of sterner stuff.

"Anyway" she went on, "I suppose I was attracted to you, once I got past the fact that you were infuriating."

He laughed.

"I'm glad we're on the same page, in wanting the same things," he spoke.

This gave her pause. She had heard that before, recently. Someone else acknowledging and rejoicing in the fact that they were on the same page and wanted the same things. And then he left. She pushed him out of her mind.

She would soon learn that The Scotsman, like her, wasn't all words, and hot air; he was action. She liked that.

It wasn't empty promises, and the stuff of fantasies. If he said he was going to do something, he did it.

Their correspondence escalated to the point where she was soon booking another trip back to Scotland, not four months after they had first met.

He invited her back to his country, and she accepted.

She wanted to explore more of Scotland anyway.

"You have to wear the kilt," she insisted.

"Aye, ok."

Recognition

One of the best perks of being a Singleton: You can travel the world, do what you want, who you want, whenever you want.

Scotland:

They did explore Scotland. He took her to all the areas, and sights she wanted to see throughout the country during the few weeks she was there, and at night, they would spend time exploring each other.

The delights that were waiting for her under his kilt were unbelievable!

They were certainly well matched in strength and passion.

She thought of the hiatus she took from men and dating, whether it was prospective suitors she passed aside, or the men she wanted simply were not interested in her (or disappeared), whatever the reasons, it led to a very long break.

Elissa Ivy Siegel

She deserved every bit of pleasure The Scotsman offered.

It was as if he worshipped her body; he loved every inch of it, thoroughly.

They would spend each night, all night, pleasuring each other completely. It was intimate and sincere at times, and aggressive and dizzying in the next turn. They enjoyed each other immensely.

She didn't remember sleeping much, but each day they'd wake with great energy and explore the countryside. And each night, they spent together.

This Scottish adventure was long overdue.

Sadly, the weeks went by too quickly.

He was staring at her now, that stare again. A look that went right through her, as if he could see all of her. Know all of her. She thought she sensed what he was going to say.
She gently put her hand to his mouth to stop the words.
Pointless words.

Recognition

"Don't tell me you love me, show me you love me," She looked at him deeply.

He lifted her around him, and took her up against the wall, as she originally requested.

Ten

Scotland

1865

"Every time he comes home, she falls pregnant," Mother began.

"That isn't true."

"Well, very nearly every time."

"They've been married for years, and now you're complaining about their way of life?" Da' asked.

Mother went on, "he's gone more than he's here. He leaves for work for months, often a year at a time. All the while, she's here raising his children. And now she's pregnant with their fourth child!"

"She never seems to mind. We all knew this was going to be their life together. We knew the nature of his profession. They seem to make it work," Da' went on, "they're not like us, together all the time, day in and day out, on and on, endless..."

She gave him a look, a side glance. Was he complaining, she thought?

"I'm not complaining," Da' went on, "but they're a very different couple, and it works for them."

"I suppose," She still looked worried.

"What is it?" he asked.

"What do you think he gets up to out there on his own?" she asked.

"Mother! What are you implying?"

"Well, you know men."

Da' thought about it.

"I don't think he'd be that stupid, our daughter would kill him," Da' joked.

Mother laughed.

"I suppose so," she agreed.

The next day on their 'walk and talk' along the loch, Da' broached the subject with his daughter.

"Your mother is concerned," he began.

"She's always concerned, what is it this time?"

"She worries, and wonders what your husband is up to when he's away from home all those months," He tried to lightly broach the topic.

His daughter didn't look surprised or upset. She nodded her head in understanding.

"She just worries that it's hard on you, staying here, left to raise the children on your own much of the time," he added.

She smiled, "she's worried about this now, we've been living like this for years."

"That's what I said," Da' agreed.

Recognition

She thought for a moment.

Then she began, "when he leaves it's like I send a piece of myself out into the world and I'm never quite sure when I'll get it back."

"It isn't easy. It is difficult for many reasons," she added.

"I love our life together, and I love our children. Though it wasn't the life I envisioned for myself," she confessed.

Da' listened.

"His work takes him all over the world now. I envy him that. I don't begrudge him his successes and opportunities. Though exploring the world was something I had hoped to do in life. However, I fell in love and raised a family instead," She smiled.

As Da' continued to listen, she explained her faith in their love, in his love for her, and in her love for him. How this love kept him coming back. That she trusts he will be a good father, and always return to his children.

"I understand there are temptations out there," She explained to her Da'.

"But I can't worry about that. It's up to him to do what he wants. I can't get dragged down in thinking about any extracurricular activities he might engage in while away," she added.

Da' looked at her in amazement. He didn't expect her to be so open.

She thought of their love together. There was an overwhelming intensity in their physical relationship, but there was also a deep intimacy between them. It was unparalleled. They could lie entangled in each other for hours caressing each other, talking, sharing. They had a connection that was unwavering. They often spoke of how they felt for one another, but more so they spoke of this connection. This feeling they each had when they were apart, and even more strongly when they were together. As if they were only actually whole when they could come together, but while they were apart they felt the other one was there with them.

Recognition

Made of the same soul.

"Don't worry Da'. He will always come back to me, to us. He loves us," she was sure of it.

"So, what did she say?" Mother asked as Da' returned home from their walk.

"Give me a minute to take off my boots woman!"

Tut.

Da' moved into the sitting room and relaxed in his chair.

"Well?" Mother persisted.

"She's fine. She trusts in their love, and she's not bothered one bit by what he might get up too while he's gone."

Mother sat and thought about it for a moment.

Da' went on, "to be honest, we're not sure why you're bring this all up now. Why are you suddenly so concerned with their lifestyle?"

"He just seemed, distant, while he was here last," Mother admitted.

"Do you know something we don't?" he pressed Mother.

"No, he didn't say anything, it was just a feeling I got, as if he was pulling away."

Da' thought about the last time he was home.

"Well, he didn't pull away far enough, she's pregnant again!" Da' spoke.

"Da'!"

"They seem fine to me," he added.

"Yes, maybe they are. We'll see when he comes home in a few months' time for the birth of his fourth child."

Mother still looked worried.

"If you're that worried, why don't you speak to him about it? You have your wee evening chats each night when he's home, ask him," Da' suggested.

"I couldn't do that! That's 'guy talk', you ask him," Mother directed.

"Me!? I'm not the one who sees any trouble between them," Da' pleaded.

"You'll do it," Mother ended the conversation and went to the kitchen to check on Cook.

He returned home, and they fell into family life without missing a beat. The children were so happy to see him, as were Mum and Da'. Cook made a special meal for his first day home.

The couple were together again. Whole.

"They seem happy," Da' began when they retired to the sitting room.

"Aye, I suppose they do," Mother spoke.

"Oh, what is it now?" asked Da'

"Nothing, she just looks very run down lately. This pregnancy is different from the others, this one is taking its toll on her."

Da' thought of his daughter.

"Do you think everything is ok? Maybe we should call a doctor to be sure," said Da'

"Aye, I'll send for him tomorrow morning. Her due date is very near, it wouldn't hurt to have the doctor close," said Mother.

Da' suddenly felt worried. He didn't fret very often; he always left the worrying to his wife. But this time, he was concerned.

Per usual, Mother was right.

Recognition

It was a very difficult birth. She spent the night in excruciating pain, accompanied by vomiting, and severe headaches.

The doctor arrived in the early hours of the morning. He took one look at her and looked panicked. This did not comfort the rest of the family.

Cook took the children to the main house and looked after them for the day.

Mother, Da', and her Country Analyst didn't move from her side.

Mother tried to assist the doctor as best she could. She would often assist as a midwife in the village for the local woman.

Da' mostly paced in the hallway.

Her Analyst, looking terrified, wouldn't let go of her hand.

She rarely panicked, but this time she was scared. Thank goodness he's home, she thought. She needed him now.

She started to hemorrhage. The doctor worked as quickly as he could, asking her to push.

But she didn't hear him. She went very pale, and then passed out.

They were able to cut the baby from her, saving him. He was a healthy baby boy. Four boys now in total. She didn't regain consciousness.

The doctor could not say how long she would be unconscious. She had lost a lot of blood, and the doctor was unsure of the outcome. For now, her pulse was strong, and her breathing was normal.

All they could do was wait.

"He won't leave her side," Mother said to Da'

"I know. He won't eat anything either," Da' added.

Recognition

"We have to pull him out of himself, it's been over a week."

They sat in silence.

"Do you think she'll be ok," Da' asked.

"She's strong. She'll wake up," Mother was sure.

Da' felt comforted. Mother was always right.

The next day Da' had to practically wrestle the Analyst away from her bed side. He got him washed and dressed and forced him to eat something before he could return to her again.

The Analyst obeyed.

Cook was an enormous help to them. She took care of all the children, including the new wee one. He, like the rest of the family, was missing his mother.

Mother spent most of her time by her daughter's bedside. Changing and washing her, and turning her as she slept, so as not to incur any bedsores.

None of them could sleep while she slumbered.

They just waited and stood watch over her. Day in, and day out.

"Did he say anything to you today?" Mother asked Da'

"No, it's like he's in a trance. At least now I can get him to eat every few hours," Da' said.

"He looked terrified during the birth. And he's looked like a lost wee lamb ever since, it's heartbreaking" Mother went on.

"We were all terrified," said Da'

"He'll come around, when she does," he added.

Mother nodded. Then she got up and joined Cook and the children in the other room. The new wee one needed some

Recognition

attention. He couldn't rely on either of his parents just now, so his grandparents would have to do. The doctor advised giving him boiled cow's milk and water to keep him fed and hydrated. Mother considered getting a wetnurse but thought better of it. So far, he seemed to be doing fine. He was a strong wee lad. Cook doted on him, and he seemed very content with her as his care giver. He was the spitting image of his father.

Mother laughed, thinking of her daughter now. She knew she would wake up and see her son, and say something like, 'I do all the work in birthing him and he pops out looking just like his Da', bloody figures.' Though Mother knew her daughter will be secretly pleased.

He was a handsome wee lad to be sure.

The doctor visited every day to check on her, and to check on the wee one.

Elissa Ivy Siegel

He tried to give the family uplifting news regarding her slumber, but there hadn't been much change.

The wee one was healthy and strong.

He was one month old.

It had been one month, one week and one day since she gave birth to the wee one.

She started to open her eyes. Everything felt heavy, and strange. She looked over and saw her husband, he was holding her hand with his head down on the bed, asleep.

Mother and Da' were propping each other up in a settee across the room, also asleep.

The wee one was in a bassinet by her bedside. She looked at him. He looked big, larger than a newborn in his first days of life. He was awake and looking at her now.

She removed her hand from her husbands' grip and lifted the wee one out of the bassinet, resting him on her chest. He was heavy, well fed by the looks of him. She held her wee lad with one arm and began stroking her husbands' dark hair with the other hand. She tried to recall what had happened. The last thing she remembered was going into labor.

She sat like this for a while, she didn't want to wake anyone.

Slowly, her husband started to wake, he was staring at her. She pushed his hair back and took his face in her hand, "hello my love," she said smiling.

He began to cry.

Mother and Da' woke and came over to the bed, they sat on the bedside and hugged her, they also had tears in their eyes.

'What is going on?' she thought.

Mother took the wee one from her and started to explain. She told her she had been asleep for over a month. That it had been an exceedingly difficult birth. Mother explained that due to complications she would not be able to have any more children. She expressed their worry in not knowing if or when she would wake up.

She looked at them all, not knowing what to say.

Mother told Da' they should give them some privacy. She took the wee one and led Da' out of the room.

The Analyst climbed into bed next to her, and rested his head on her chest, weeping.

She held onto him tightly. Caressing the back of his head, and the length of his back, trying to soothe him.

"I'm ok, my love, I feel fine," she went on, "I'm so sorry to give you all such a fright."

He just held onto her tightly.

They stayed like this for a long while.

Eventually, he steadied himself and asked her if she needed anything.

Recognition

"I'm starving!" she confessed, "will you make me one of your steak pies!?"

He started to laugh, "I'll make you anything you want."

"I love you," he added.

"I love you more," she returned.

"I can't ever lose you," He said seriously.

She pulled him in again, "you won't lose me. And I won't ever lose you."

He gave her a long, sweet kiss.

They never did lose each other. Not for a very, very long time, when in their old age, he slipped away peacefully in her arms, with his family surrounding his bedside.

Now, when they were ready to get out of bed after her long slumber, she tried to stand, but it was difficult. She was shocked by how weak her legs felt. He scooped her up, and lifted her in his arms, carrying her to the kitchen table. She was holding onto his neck and laughing as they approached Mother and Da'.

When they entered the kitchen, she looked at her new wee son, and said, turning to her husband, "He is the very image of you. Bloody typical, I do all the work in birthing him, and he pops out looking just like you!" she teased.

Mother laughed.

In the next few weeks, Mother put her on a strict health regime. She was to start off eating light foods only, to get her system used to solid food. And she would move daily to gain the strength back in her limbs.

The steak pie would have to wait.

Recognition

Da' and daughter resumed their daily 'walk and talk's' along the loch.

At first, she had to take Da's' arm and lean on him to get down the path, but each day she got stronger, and soon she was bounding down the path at her normal strength and speed.

One afternoon, Da' started, "we were all very scared while you were, asleep."

"I know Da', but I'm much better now."

"When things were at their worst, during the birth, your husband looked terrified," he went on, "I was sure that if anything happened to you, he would have died right along with you."

"Da'!"

"He wouldn't leave your side, we had to force him from your bedside to bathe and eat. He was in utter shock."

"He wouldn't have died with me," she insisted, "he would have pulled himself together, with help from you and Mum, and he would have taken care of our children."

"I'm just so thankful it didn't come to that," he spoke.

"I know Da'," She said, giving him a hug.

Later when Da' returned to the house, he went to speak with Mother in the sitting room.

"How was your walk?" Mother began.

"Good. She's much stronger, she bounced right back!" said Da'

"Aye, she's made of strong stuff, our girl."

Da' smiled.

"Did you engage in some witty banter with your wee boyfriend?" he asked.

Recognition

Ever since The Analyst and Mother started having their talks, Da' and daughter teased her that he was her boyfriend.

"He's not my boyfriend! He is doing well. And he had some interesting news," she said, pleased as punch.

"Aye, go on then."

"He asked for a permanent, local commission at work. He will not be traveling for long periods of time, or long distances. They agreed to give him this position, which will keep him close to his family. He will be home for good now," Mother informed him.

"He has had quite a scare," Da' spoke.

"Aye, but I think beyond that, he has realized that he has missed too much time with his family. It's time to come home," she declared.

"Do you still want me to talk to him?" Da' asked.

"Talk to him about what?"

"You said I should speak to him, about the distance you noticed when he was traveling last," Da' clarified.

"Oh no, that's all sorted now. When he returned this time, the distant feeling I was getting from him had gone," Mother spoke.

"You could have told me woman! I nearly said something to him," Da' said shaking his head.

"Well, I'm glad you feel that his distance has gone," he added.

"Everything will be fine from here on out," She predicted.

(Although with Mother it is never a prediction, it's a guarantee.)

As the wee one got older, he became his father's shadow. He followed his Da' everywhere.

When he was hungry, when he needed a wash, when he was hurt, he only wanted Dada.

Recognition

Never Mumma.

It stung a bit that he always wanted to run to her husband for any need. Though she was also happy they had this connection. Her husband didn't get to experience this with their first three children. But now that he was home permanently, they settled into a new way of life. The family life. And the wee one only wanted Dada.

One afternoon, while Da', her husband, and all four of the children went to the market, she was in the sitting room speaking to Mother.

"Is the wee one still following in his Dada's footsteps?" Mother asked.

"Aye, the Wee Shite," she teased.

"Stop calling him that, he'll think it's his name!" said Mother.

"I'm thinking of having it legally changed," she joked.

"You're terrible!"

They both laughed.

She continued, "he is still his father's son. He looks like him, he moves like him, he even laughs like him. The only difference is that my son doesn't have the scar on his ear like his father,"

Mother smiled.

"It's good for them both. They've bonded," Mother said.

"In truth, I love it. It is wonderful that My Love is getting the full experience of parenthood, but it would be nice if the wee one didn't wriggle out of my arms to run to Dada all the bloody time."

She went on, "however, it is delightful to see them together. Two peas in a pod."

The other three children were much closer to her than her husband. He was away for much of their childhoods, and they always went to Mum for everything. They still did.

Recognition

Their first child, the eldest, looked like her. Tall, blonde hair, blue eyes. He was a lovely lad, and he was turning into a wonderful young man. He was strong and fiery, but he had a kind heart. Like his mother.

Their two middle children, who were born barely a year apart, looked like a mix of both Mum and Dad. They were close in age, but they were total opposites. The second eldest always had his nose in a book, always studying, always learning. Their third child was a free spirit, he loved nature and drawing and creating things.

And of course, the wee one. Dada's boy. He was both creative and studious, as well as strong. He loved play and sport and excelled at everything he did.

They were blessed with kind, loving, beautiful children.

Soon after the men returned from the market, Cook went to work making them a grand feast. They were having a big family dinner this night.

Da' and daughter, and the eldest headed out for their walk along the loch before supper. Surprisingly, the wee one wanted to join them. Though it wasn't that much of a surprise, the only person he loved as much as he loved Dada, was his Grand-Dada. He raced out of the house and pushed his way between his mother and his Grand-Dada', so that he could hold Grand-Dada's hand.

She shook her head and laughed, then sped up to catch up to her eldest son.

It was a beautiful evening.

Supper was delicious, per usual. The family had a wonderful time. Cook joined them at dinner regularly, the wee one always sat by her, his other best friend.

She looked over at her husband and took his hand. She leaned in to kiss him. Suddenly, she felt so grateful, and so incredibly happy in this moment. Holding onto her Love and surrounded by her family. They are all happy, healthy, and loved.

Recognition

While in the sitting room later that evening, Da' began, "our lass looked very happy tonight."

"Aye, so did her husband. They're settling into family life very happily. I was worried that it would be a tough transition, but they are more than content with their new way of life," said Mother.

"It's true, I expected it to be a big change for them. They each valued their independence in their own ways, while he was away all those years. I thought it would be difficult for them to transition to the close knit, ordinary family life, being with each other day in and day out," Da' spoke.

"They look like they did after they were first married," said Mother.

"More in love than ever," Da' agreed.

"Everything will be grand from here on out," Mother insisted. (Mother was never wrong.)

Eleven
The United States of America
2022

A society grows great when old men plant trees, the shade of which they know they will never sit. – Greek Proverb

She rarely saw this selflessness in people these days. Had times changed? Had people changed? How did we all get so self-obsessed? She was guilty of self-obsession at times, but she tried to do her best, to be thoughtful, to take others into account.

To show respect and instill dignity in every human being.

There are good people in the world. She was just having trouble finding them.

She certainly wasn't seeing much selflessness in her dating pool. This wasn't because she has a dim view of humanity,

Recognition

she truly tried to give everyone the benefit of the doubt. And yet, it was often met with disappointment.

It was disheartening.

She heard someone reference that proverb, and it made her think of the men in her family.

She was, quite literally, sitting underneath a tree that they had planted many years ago.

They were not perfect. But they were incredibly kind, good men. The type of people to help, not only their friends, family, and neighbors, but also the type of people to help total strangers. Help anyone in need, even when they themselves were in need. She saw them complete acts that were utterly selfless. Her dad, and her avuncular. It was the best description for him. This close family friend that was family, not by blood, but in every other possible way.

The two male figures in her life, whom even when they had their own troubles, were always lending a helping hand. She could scarcely remember a time when they weren't helping a friend or neighbor in the community.

This, she thought, was true heroism.

Not just the men in her family, the woman as well. Selfless.

Long time neighbors and family friends who are with you until the end.

She recalled the friends and families she grew up with in her hometown. Her classmates, and friends she had met along the way. They were kind souls. People who would always lend an ear, show support, give a helping hand. These were the people she grew up with, and she was grateful they were still in her life today. Childhood friends, now adults. Though not much had changed between them. Even if they don't see each other for months or years, when they come together, it's as if they had never been apart. The community she was part of, and they were a part of her.

Recognition

And today, when she returns to her old neighborhood, they are still there, to welcome her with open arms, and a friendly face.

A tree planted, providing shelter and shade.

It was home.

She was incredibly lucky to have had a good home, and a kind family. It very nearly didn't happen. She had been adopted at a very young age. She started out in the world utterly alone.

Alone, and uncared for, in the first weeks and months of life.

But it wasn't long before they found her.

A family, complete.

They had plenty of struggles over the years, but she wouldn't have changed a thing.

She always hated the phrase, 'blood is thicker than water'.

To her, this phrase couldn't be further from the truth. Her entire family from start to finish, was water, none of them were blood. And yet, they were stronger than any family she knew, this included her family of friends. The people we invite into our lives, to become family. Fully supported by one another. Connected by love. Blood had nothing to with it.

"Stop being hurtful!" she said to no one in particular.

She lived alone, and now she's watching the news; the headlines were horrific.

Singleton's often talk to themselves; don't worry, it's normal.

This is not a time to be hurtful to anyone, she thought. People are killing each other in the streets. And yet, we continue to

Recognition

hurt the people who are closest to us, those we care about the most.

Tearing each other apart and tearing one another down.

Tensions are high, and the stress is overwhelming. But this is not a time to be hurtful to one another. True kindness was becoming a rarity.

She turned off the television and went to get ready for bed.

It was spring, but the farmhouse still felt cold. She took a hot shower, put on some cozy pajamas, and climbed under the covers.

It had been a long day, a long week… a long few months.

She thought about him. The Ghost.

She wasn't feeling lonely exactly, but she would have liked to have someone to talk to when life got stressful. It was one of the things she missed most about him, their long conversations. They used to talk about everything, and she wished she still had the option to reach out and discuss their lives, and their day-to-day. To talk about world events, to have a distraction from such events, or to reach out and see how he was feeling.

Earlier on, something would happen in the day, and she would think, 'I have to tell him about this, or that'. Often, she would think, 'he would find this hilarious; I'll have to send him a text.' etc...

There were many things she wanted to tell him over these last months. Many occasions she had hoped to share, photos and stories she wished she could send him.

But she didn't have that option any longer.

Thinking about how much she missed him, she drifted off to sleep.

Recognition

Twelve

Boston

1775

Silence is debilitating.

She created this silence between them, and now she wasn't sure how to end it.

How do we come back from the silence?

After his disappearing act while he was on his "top secret" mission, she hadn't spoken to him since his return.

They were still working in the same unit. Though she had chosen to work with the other boys in these last weeks. She spent her days ignoring him, working with her team of boys, and paying frequent visits to The Caretaker who had helped her when she was in search of him.

Shortly after he returned, she went to tell The Caretaker that her friend had been found, alive and well. Visiting him at the morgue had become a regular part of her routine. She would often bring him an apple from the cart, or some lunch, if she had time between running her errands for the unit.

"I'm very glad to hear that your friend is well," The Caretaker spoke.
She had brought a packed lunch to share on this visit. She thought he could use a break from all the death.
"Thank you, I am happy he's well, but I can't help but be angry with him," she said, biting into her half of the sandwich.
"He gave you quite a scare, I know."
"I suppose so," she said, begrudgingly. She didn't like to show her fear.
"It took great courage to come here and look for him amongst this lot," he said pointing to the building behind them.
"It takes great courage to deal with this lot each day, and still remain as kind as you."
She had wanted to tell him how kind he was on her first visit to the morgue but didn't get the chance to do so; it felt like a

thing unfinished, not being able to say it, and she hated a thing unfinished.

The Caretaker gave her a blushed smile.

"I understand your anger; he should have contacted you to let you know he wasn't in any danger, but don't you think it's time to let the anger go?" he asked.

"We haven't spoken in weeks. I don't know where to begin; I don't know how to come back from the silence," she admitted.

"You just speak, that's all," he simplified.

She nodded in understanding, though she still wasn't quite sure what to say.

That night, in the barracks, they were lying in silence.

It was a strange occurrence, ignoring someone you care about so deeply.

Although they were side by side, the distance between them had grown too great.

A feeling of emptiness came over her as they lay there, back-to-back.

Recognition

She rolled over and looked at him. She couldn't tell if he was asleep. He was curled up under the covers with his back to her, silent.

What could she say? She lay there for some time trying to think of the words.

After a while, she reached out and placed her hand on his back.

He rolled over and took her hand in his.

And just like that, without saying a word, the silence was broken.

They never spoke of his "Top Secret" mission.

The next morning, they were back together. Complete.

Friends, partners, patriots.

Although tensions were high among the barracks, they didn't have any errands or assignments to complete this day. They decided to go out for a walk to talk about the events of the last few weeks. He had been working very closely with The General. He told her as much as he was allowed to share of their work together. She too had information to share, the errands she and the boys were completing. They sensed war was on the rise.

As they walked and talked, the air turned bitter cold around them, though they didn't seem to notice.

After catching up with each other, she brought him to meet her friend, The Caretaker.

He was pleased to see them both speaking again. The Caretaker could see how much they cared for each other. It pleased him to see they had put the anger behind them. The three of them sat and had a light lunch together.

As they walked away from the morgue after their visit, he began, "how did you meet him?"

She looked at him, not fully ready to relive that story, but she went on in any case, "I went to the morgue to look for you

Recognition

when you were missing. The Caretaker allowed me to view the bodies, to see if any of them matched your description."

He gave her a solemn look and continued to listen.

"There was a boy that matched your build and hair color, but his face was beaten so badly, that I couldn't tell if it was you. And then I saw the boy's ear."

"His ear?" he questioned.

"He didn't have the scar on his ear. Like yours" she reached up and gave his ear a gentle tug.

He smiled. "Ah, I see."

"Anyway, The Caretaker was kind enough to keep me informed if anyone of your description arrived at the morgue," she went on, "he's a very kind man; I would often go back to speak with him, and bring him an apple, or prepare a lunch from time to time."

"You didn't bring him stolen apples, did you!?" he teased.

She laughed and pushed him off his footing in a playful manner, "no! I paid for them this time."

They both laughed.

As they briskly walked to the barracks, she glanced over at him. His face was red with the cold, though his eyes were shining bright, and he was smiling. He's happy, she thought. In this moment, she realized how difficult her silence was on him. She was sorry to have caused him any pain. In any other case, she would have just lost her temper, exploded in anger, the instant he returned from his mission, and that would have been it. But with him it was different. She couldn't let the anger out. At first, she thought she was sparing him by keeping her temper, but now she saw that the silence was far worse.

She wished she could reach out to touch him now, but they were too close to the barracks.

In the broad light of day, someone would see her (him). Sometimes being a boy was hard, she thought.

In the next weeks, he continued his work with The General, and she stayed with the boys in their efforts for the unit. Though each night, they'd come together and share the

Recognition

events of their day and offer as much information as they could regarding the growing tensions.

Always falling asleep, hand in hand.

She continued her visits with The Caretaker when time would allow. She learned that he was originally from England, though he had spent most of his adult life here in Boston. He considered Boston his true home. She understood. She didn't harbor the feelings for the British that her fellow Patriot harbored. She decided then not to tell her companion that The Caretaker was English. The Caretaker had a wife and daughter who had died many years ago, due to illness. He told her that his daughter would have been close to her age now.

"I like to think she would have been a lovely young lady. Just like you," he spoke.

She looked at him in shock.

"I know you're a girl," he added.

A look of panic came over her face.

"It's ok, I would never tell anyone."

She eased a bit. It had become increasingly difficult these last months to hide her curves, and the ever-growing beauty in her reflection.

He went on, "your young man also knows, doesn't he?" The Caretaker asked.

"He's not my young man," she corrected, "yes, he's known since we first met."

"Oh, isn't he? My mistake," he said, looking at her, smiling.

She blushed and turned away.

"Your secret is safe with me," he went on, "I expect it is safer to be a boy, when you're on your own on these streets."

"Yes, it was. Although, I expect I'm not fooling anyone any longer," she assumed.

"No, don't think that. In my profession, I have studied anatomy quite closely. I think it was easier for me to pick up on your wraps, and additional padding. I think you can still pass as a boy," he tried to console.

She smiled, "I hope so. I don't think The General would be too pleased to know he had a girl in his regimen all this time."

Recognition

"Also, I saw the way your young man looks at you. I could see instantly that you were a girl when I saw the look in his eye," he added.

She blushed, "he is not my young man!"

"Ok, ok," he smiled.

As she walked back to the barracks, she was lost in thought. Would others start to see what The Caretaker saw? Perhaps, they were too close, she and her Patriot.

She didn't see the figure approaching her, he brushed past her too closely, hitting her shoulder and knocking her around to face him as he passed. Her cap nearly fell off, but she caught it.

A quick glance was exchanged before he turned and walked on.

For a moment, she sensed a recognition between them. Did he remember her?

Heart pounding, she turned and hurried back to the barracks.

It was the Redcoat that had set upon her at the pond last autumn.

She desperately scanned the barracks for her companion. Spotting him, she grabbed him by the lapels and led him into a secluded tent on the outskirts of the camp. She felt such an urgency to tell him of the encounter with the Redcoat, that she pulled him into the tent with great force.

This force thrusts them face to face now. Close. She looked up at him, their eyes locked on each other. They were staring most ardently. Their bodies nearly touching.

For a moment, she was speechless. Staring. He stepped closer to her.

She steadied herself by placing her hands on his chest. He leaned in.

Everything seemed to be moving in slow motion. She had forgotten what was so urgent...

After a time, coming back to herself, she shook the array of emotions she was feeling aside.

Recognition

"Stop!" she said, pushing his body from hers, "I have to tell you something."

He let go of her and looked at her again. She looked shaken now, scared.

"What is it?" he asked, concerned.

"I bumped into the Redcoat from the pond. I think he recognized me."

"He saw you as a boy?" he clarified.

"Yes, but the look he gave me, I think he knows," she said.

"And you're worried he's going to expose you as a girl?" he asked.

"Yes, among other things."

He looked at her for more clarification.

She hadn't told her companion, but the Redcoat knew more about her than her true gender.

He was growing suspicious as he waited for her to clarify. Stepping away from her now, a flash of anger went across his face.

"Were you with that DAMN, Redcoat while I was gone!?" he demanded.

"What? NO! That day at the pond was the first day I had ever set eyes on him," she reassured.

He calmed down, "ok, then why are you so concerned?"

"It's not as if The General is going to be pleased to find out that he's had a girl in his regiment all this time. He will kick me out and then I'll be on the streets again."

"That won't happen. If they kick you out, I'll leave with you," he said matter-of-factly.

"You can't do that! You're The General's best man. He is brining you up in the ranks, you can't leave now!" she pleaded.

"It will be fine. Whatever happens, I will take care of you," he promised.

'Take care of her?', she thought with a hint of anger, but she let it slide.

Instead, she stepped towards him, taking him into an embrace, and resting her head on his chest.

A few weeks had passed since their discussion about the Redcoat.

Recognition

She started to feel a slight sense of security again.
Perhaps the Redcoat wouldn't reveal her true identity after all.

She and her companion were looking forward to the warmer months ahead, spring was upon them, and they were dreaming of their days spent swimming in the pond. They couldn't wait to get back there and have their time together.

As they rose one morning, hand in hand, they heard a commotion going on in the front square.
They dressed and made their way out to see what was going on.
Her heart nearly stopped; it was the Redcoat.
She looked at her companion in fear.
Before either of them could say or do anything The General was approaching them.
"You two, follow me," he directed.
The General led the way with the Redcoat close on his heels.
The other two followed, as ordered.

They went into one of the buildings the generals and commanders use for official business.

The General stepped towards her companion and asked him to join him at the front of the room.

He looked at her, and then complied.

The Redcoat approached her, and grabbed her by the arm, leading her to the middle of the room. A British commander and several other Redcoats were present.

She looked at her companion. He gave her a reassuring look. Strength.

Without any formalities, the Redcoat stepped forward and removed her cap. Her golden blonde hair fell down her back and around her face.

She looked at The General. He was in utter shock. Wide eyed, thinking of all the missions she had carried out – a girl!

The Redcoat gripped her tighter, pulling her arm, "there's more" he said.

Oh no, here it comes, she thought.

"She is a British citizen" The Redcoat informed them.

Recognition

She looked at her companion now. She watched a wave of emotions pass over his face: disbelief, confusion, realization, anger, sadness, a lot more anger...

He saw by the look on her face that the Redcoat was not lying.

She gave him a pleading look. Why doesn't he say something, she thought? He could speak up and defend her. Come to her aid. Say something on her behalf. He remained silent.

She had hurt him. Her omission. Her lie. He felt betrayed. She looked away; she couldn't take the look in his eyes any longer.

The Redcoat was claiming treason.

Treason! She thought.

She started to defend herself, though she wasn't sure who she was addressing. The Brits, The General?

"I don't even remember England. I was raised here. Boston has been my home since I was a baby. I don't know any other home," she thought she wasn't helping herself against the claim on treason, as she added, "I'm a Patriot."

The General stepped forward and consulted the British commander in chief.

They spoke in private while the Redcoat kept an ever-tighter grip on her arm.

Everyone waited.

She hoped The General was speaking on her behalf. Treason after all, is the ultimate punishment. Did she really deserve that? She glanced at her companion. Her Patriot returned her glance with hate in his eyes.

She felt the tears welling up, but she pushed them back. She could not cry in front of them, no matter the outcome.

The Redcoat leaned in, his breath brushing her neck, as he said in a cruel tone, "your beau doesn't look too pleased."

The General and The Commander returned.

Her heart started to pound. She moved closer to the Redcoat. She wasn't sure why, he was the only person close to her at the moment, she supposed.

Recognition

The Commander spoke, "we have agreed that treason is too high a price to pay," he went on, "this was your grievance", he said addressing the Redcoat holding her, "you may decide her punishment, but it must not be death," he concluded.
She thought that still left a lot of room for some very severe punishment indeed.
She looked at the Redcoat now. He did not look forgiving.
He increased his grip again and forced her to her knees.
Gritting her jaw, she didn't make a sound.
"If you want to be a Boston Boy so badly, you should look the part," he said, retrieving a knife from his boot.
He grabbed a chunk of her hair and started shaving it off in chunks.
She could see her lovely, golden locks falling to the floor in front of her.
He pulled and cut with such a force, it cut her scalp in several places. Blood started to rush down her face. She didn't cry.
She stayed still until he was finished.
She was almost completely bald, with small patches of hair and blood mapping her scalp.

He pulled her to her feet, squaring off with her. Taking off his coat, he challenged her to a fight.

"If you're such a tough soldier, let see what you've got."

She looked at his commander, and the rest of the room. No one seemed inclined to stop the Redcoat. Seriously, she thought, are we really settling this with fisticuffs?

She squared up to him, getting in his face now, "aren't you afraid you'll be beat by a girl?"

He stepped back and landed such a blow with the back of his hand to her left cheek that she went crashing to the ground in the thud. She had forgotten how strong he was, when she was in his grip by the pond all those months ago. This was an opponent she could not beat.

But she wouldn't back down.

Dizzy, and wiping the blood from her eyes, she got to her feet and looked at him. Her brow narrowed, her eyes – fiery, her face flashed crimson, and she charged at him with all of her force. He grabbed her as she landed a quick upper cut. Bloodied, he landed backwards, with her on top of him. He hit his head on the ground, hard. It stunned him for a moment, and she wasted no time. She continued to wallop him, from a straddled position, pinning him to the ground. His head clearing, he threw her off of him, again with great force.

She got to her feet as quick as she could and landed a strong, forceful downward kick to his knee cap. He yelled out in pain but didn't go down. He was really angry now, she thought. She braced for impact. He came at her, landing hit, after hit, after hit. He got in some damaging body shots, one to the ribs, one to her left kidney, and another back hand that put her down, hard. She couldn't see for the blood in her eyes. Everything hurt.

He wasn't just strong; he knew how to fight. She was in trouble now. Writhing on the floor.

He kneeled next to her, and pulled her up by her lapels, her body limp on the ground, he pulled her face close to his. Blood was dripping from his face, she was happy about that, she had gotten a few licks in. His blood dripped onto her mixing with her own.

"Have you had enough yet?" he asked.

"No, have you?" she spat back.

He was really angry now, she thought. Why did she always have to push it one step too far?

In a rage, he yanked her off the floor, she felt as if she had taken flight. He brought her down again, with a slam. She held onto him and started coughing up blood. He wouldn't stop. He was thrashing her around like she was a rag doll. She heard something crack. She was fairly certain it was her. 'He's going to tear me in half,' she thought. Just as he was about to land another blow, one of the British soldiers stepped in and pulled the Redcoat off of her. "Enough!" he yelled.

The Redcoat backed off and stepped away.

The British soldier looked at her with a kind, compassionate stare; he offered her his hand.

She took it, and he helped her to her feet. She nodded at him, a thank you.

She looked around the room, no one in the room showed any concern for her, except this British soldier, not even her companion. They all just stared at her and The Redcoat like they were the main event. Nothing but sport.

She glanced at the kind soldier again and fell into his arms. Her limbs didn't seem to be working properly.

He held her and propped her up. Resting against his chest, she glanced over at the Redcoat. He was bruised and bloodied, clothes torn, and looking completely disheveled. She started to smile.

The Redcoat, angered at seeing her smile, charged at her and the soldier.

"ENOUGH!" The Commander ordered.

The Redcoat stopped. He looked at The Commander, wiping the blood from his face with the back of his hand, he said, "I want her deported. Let that be her punishment."

Deported, she thought, hanging onto the soldier, to England!?

"Now get her out of my sight," The Redcoat added.

The British soldier sat her down on a chair at the back of the room.

She tried to look around the room. She saw The General and her companion leave without so much as a glance back. Her heart broke. She suddenly felt very alone.

The Redcoat stormed out, followed by the other soldiers.

Her kind soldier remained, as did The Commander.

She looked at him now. He was about to explain the details of her deportation.

After the sentence was passed, the soldier took her into the washroom to get her cleaned up.

With all that was thrown at her today, she didn't shed one single tear.

The soldier was explaining that he had medical training, and he would be looking over her injuries. She didn't protest. She was too weak.

He began to take her clothes off and found the layers of wrapping that diminished her curves.

He started to unwarp them, "I think these may have saved your life today," he said, continuing to work and unwrap the padding.

Recognition

"They saved me many times over the years," she spoke, blankly staring off past him.

He nodded in understanding.

He was pleased to see that her injuries were actually quite minor, considering the beating she had taken today. The wraps took much of the impact.

He continued to clean up her cuts and mend her bruises. Then after undressing her completely, he lifted her, and put her into the bath.

Again, she didn't put up a fight. There was no fight left.

She sank into the warm water and closed her eyes.

He left the room while she finished her bath and got dressed.

After she was clean and dressed, she felt better. If it was possible to feel better after the day she just had.

She emerged from the bathroom, and the soldier was there waiting for her.

He would be escorting her on her journey back to The United Kingdom.

The Commander didn't trust that she would get on the ship.

He wasn't wrong, she thought.

She was content that her escort would be the kind soldier.

She was grateful for that, at least.

He agreed to meet her at the pier the following morning to board the ship.

He reminded her that if she did not appear at the ship when it was ready to set sail a warrant would be made for her arrest.

She told him she understood.

He put a hand on her shoulder.

She looked at him, he really was very kind, she thought.

"You'll be ok," he reassured her.

She forced a smile.

"I'll see you in the morning," he concluded, and then he left.

She left the building and stepped out onto Tory Row.

Her companion was standing across the street.

From their positions on opposite sides of the road, they stood and stared at each other for an awfully long time.

Recognition

She could see how angry he was with her. He was hurt. Why didn't she ever tell him, she thought? She would tell him everything, so why did she hide this from him?

She was afraid to lose him. That is why she never told him. She wished she could go to him, to tell him that she was still the same person.

She was still his person.

But he turned and walked away from her.

She watched the back of him until he was out of view.

Everything felt broken. Everything was broken.

Not having anywhere to go, she walked towards the common. She sat on the bench and tried to pull herself together.

What had she lost, after all, she tried to console herself?

She touched her head, losing her hair… it would grow back.

Losing her country… she would find a new one.

Losing him. She started to cry.

Somehow, through all of the sobbing, she drifted off to sleep on a park bench.

She was woken sometime later by a man racing through the streets on horseback. She couldn't quite make out who it was, though she thought he was vaguely familiar.

"THE BRITISH ARE COMING!" he shouted.

And so it begins, she thought.

Recognition

Thirteen
The United States of America
2022

Someone had asked her how her dating pool was lately.

"Full of guppies," she replied.

They laughed.

Her dating pool, past and present, was often full of guppies. Not everyone in the pool, but most. They all thought they were big fish, but she could see them clearly. Guppies.

(She excludes The Scotsman. The Scotsman is a big fish, but he's a separate story.)

Recognition

The latest Guppy is messaging her and spinning a story she knows full well is total bullshit. But she lets him carry-on in any case.

If the guppies feel as though they need to lie to her, or embellish, or try to appease her with fallacies, she allows it. She allows them to spew their bullshit, and she never expects them to make good on their promise. For the most part, they're happy with this arrangement.

It's a win – win. They feel 'big' in making these promises, and she gets free of them when the promises are not fulfilled.

Another one bites the dust. Win.

Flush.

She often wondered how much of her brief time with her Ghost was utter bullshit.

To his credit, he spun a story better than most.

Even though a few of his actions were guppy-like, he wasn't a guppy. She wasn't sure what he was, but he couldn't be a guppy.

Whatever his intensions, it didn't matter now.

Thinking of the dating pool, she witnessed these fallacies throughout, with the people she was meeting, the people her friends were meeting. Bullshit, after bullshit, after bullshit.

Lately, many of her friends were calling with one relationship problem after another. Friends who were married, friends who were dating, fellow singletons. Each and every conversation was focused on their relationships and how poorly they were being treated.

She loved being there for her friends and didn't mind that the conversations were mainly focused on their most recent relationship woes, the disheartening thing was the content. No one seemed to be in a good place relationship-wise. The way people were treating each other was horrendous.

Recognition

Which often begs the question: Why fucking bother?

People lying to each other.

People cheating on each other.

People living in such a state of entitlement that they can't see or appreciate what is before them.

People trying to juggle several sidepieces at a time.

People too afraid to make a real connection, so they'd rather spin a story, than dive into something real.

People hurting each other.

People who don't keep their word.

People too self-obsessed to even ask you about your day, and genuinely listen to the answer.

People ghosting each other.

People backstabbing one another.

People who don't really know themselves, and therefore, have nothing to offer.

People desperate for someone to understand them, and yet, they won't let anyone in.

People with no self-awareness.

The list of grievances was endless.

All she could do was listen. She didn't have the answers. She would often try to console by saying: "Someone out there must be getting it right. There must be good, solid relationships existing somewhere." Maybe it gave them hope, maybe not.

"Complain all you want, and never apologize," She would say to her friends.

She always believed complaining or 'venting' was incredibly therapeutic. There was never any need to apologize. No matter how many times she had heard the list of complaints.

On too many occasions, she discovered that the fantasy was always better than the reality, when it came to being with someone.

Recognition

So, she stood up in the shallow end, and walked out of the pool.

She refers to 'people' treating each other horrendously. It is not just men. For the record, women are assholes too. When the men in her circle of friends were hurt by women, she would ponce on those women like a lioness defending her cubs.

She recalled an incident years ago when she came to the aid of one of her cubs. They were in their early 20's and this friend of hers was a bit of a ladies' man. He had been dating a girl who had a reputation for making some very serious trouble for the men she dated who dumped her.

Knowing her friend as she did, and knowing this girls' past behavior, she invited the girl out to dinner.

Elissa Ivy Siegel

The Dinner:

"Order anything you'd like, it's on me," she began.

They engaged in idle chit-chat until the waiter took their order.

She continued, "I asked you to dinner because I wanted to discuss your past behavior with the men you've dated."

The girl, who we will refer to as CB (Crazy Bitch), took a sip of wine, and stared at her like a deer caught in headlights.

Now that she had her full attention, she went on, "I know you made some serious allegations towards the men who have dumped you in the past, and as your father is a high ranking official in this city, he found ways to make certain charges stick… even though I know many of your claims were false. I don't condone my friend's behavior, but he is mine, he is family. And I defend my family to the death. Do you understand me?"

"Yes."

Recognition

"He goes through women like water, and soon he will dump you. I don't want any trouble at our doorstep when this happens. If there is any trouble, I will come after you, and I will come after your father. As powerful as you think daddy is, he is nothing compared to the powerful people I have access too."

CB was letting this all sink in, silently.

"Look at my face. You will not win if you take me on," she added.

"I understand," CB uttered.

"Now, don't get me wrong, I actually like you quite a bit. I am not threatening you. I consider us friends, new friends, but friends all the same. But as I said, he is family. And no one brings any trouble to mine. On the upside, as our friendship grows, I will absolutely go to bat like this for you one day - if you ever need me. And don't think that he's going to get off easy. I'll be speaking to him about his behavior, but he doesn't need an additional lesson from you or your father, got it?"

"Yes."

"Good, now let's eat. This looks delicious!"

In truth, she never knew anybody. She didn't have any connections in the big city. It was all a lot of hot air. But sometimes, you need to scare the bullies. You have to be crazier than the crazy, or at least make them believe you are. However, if trouble did land at their door, she would have moved heaven and earth to make good on her promise.

Two weeks later, he broke up with CB. And they all continued on in peace.

When someone cheats on her friends, or leaves them for someone else, it makes her cringe when her friends call her up to bash the new woman their ex is dating. They continue to praise the man, 'he's a good guy' they will say, but 'what does he see in that girl?' 'She's ugly'. 'She doesn't have any personality'. 'She's a bitch. etc.' It is sad really, this misplaced anger.

Women beating each other down verbally.

Little do people realize - their partner meeting someone else was the best possible outcome.

As women, we must stop tearing each other down, especially over a man. What an utter waste of energy, time, and emotion?

Genuinely complimenting and raising people up is true confidence.

'Women' genuinely complimenting each other is a thing of beauty. Not compliments spoken through gritted teeth, not half-assed compliments, not back-handed compliments.

Truth in praise lifts us up. It lifts both the person receiving the complement, and the person offering it.

Elissa Ivy Siegel

A few years back while on a business trip in L.A., she was stepping out of an Uber, and laughing her usual booming laugh. She had just told the Uber driver a joke, and in typical fashion, laughed at her own joke. (She thinks she's hilarious.)

As she closed the car door and turned to go to the office, a woman looking so utterly fabulous that she must have been a movie star, approached her and grabbed her arm.

Grabbing the woman's arm in return she said, "are you alright, Love?"

She thought perhaps the woman grabbed onto her for support.

"I am fine. I just want to tell you how beautiful you are!"

"Thank you! That is so nice of you to say but look at you! You're fabulous from head to toe, you look like a film star!" she returned.

The woman smiled, perfect teeth and all. "You absolutely exude confidence, it is beautiful."

Recognition

"Oh, thank you! You know, I'm from Boston, we're all like this," she joked.

The woman laughed and told her to have a nice day. And she did.

She never forgot this encounter, not because the compliment was so lovely, it was, but the true beauty was the mutual recognition and confidence each woman had in giving each other a genuine compliment, for no other reason than to tell each other what they were thinking.

Raising each other up.

Sometimes the occasion calls for directness, and taking the bully down a peg, and other times it calls for genuine kindness, and fulfillment.

Pick your battles. And give your compliments genuinely, not freely.

Singletons are made in strength.

Elissa Ivy Siegel

They are fiercely independent, outgoing, adventurous, and charismatic. (Oh no what a minute, that's my horoscope! #Aries)

The singleton can be all of these things, and they are so much more.

They have persevered and adapted to a certain way of life, all on their own.

They value the people in their lives because they know and understand the worth of those people.

At the end of a very tough day, they come home to an empty house, and can only rely on themselves to save the day and make it better.

They are bold, often without fear, as they dive into a new adventure. Relying on their own strength to see them through whatever that adventure brings to their life.

The downfall: Due to this instilled strength, they often see weakness in others very clearly.

Recognition

She had mentioned to the most recent Guppy that she could see people for what they truly are, see through the bullshit, as it were.

"Oh, yeah, go on then, what do see in me?"

They should never ask, she thought, because she would tell.

She looked at him and thought about it for a moment. She hadn't known him long, but his reputation was gaining traction around town. She didn't like to engage in idle gossip, but she could see that many of the stories had some truth to them.

"Well, I could be wrong," she says this to soften the blow, "but I think you're conflicted."

"You're split between the person you are and the person you portray to others. We all do this to an extent, but your true self is hidden most of the time. You can be charismatic, and charming to get what you want, but once you've obtained the desired result, you move on. There is never any follow through, no substance. People are drawn to your charm and friendly personality, but in the end they will find out you're, what I would call, 'fluff'. You're 'seemingly kind', you offer kindness and caring in your words, but never in your actions. Your self-indulgence is damaging, not just to the people in your life, but to yourself as well, though you don't see it. I personally believe everyone should be a little selfish, but you've made it an art form. You will do what you have to, to get what you want, no matter the cost. In your relationships, in your career, in your community. You would throw your own mother under a bus if it meant you could get what you wanted. The exuded charm helps you to cover these self-obsessed tendencies. People rarely see the true you, by the time they have a clear picture, you've already moved on. You won't make any apologies, and you won't make amends, the only time you'll do so is for personal gain."

She could see him glazing over now, so she stopped.

"How was that? Accurate?" she asked.

He was silent.

Recognition

"I thought so." As she got up to leave, she added, "I would tell you to take good care of yourself, but I know you always do."

Smiling, she thought to herself, 'people always wonder why I'm single; it's because they ask me to describe them'.

#flushtheguppies

(No fish were harmed, or flushed, in the writing of this story.)

Elissa Ivy Siegel

Fourteen

England

1960

(In a village just outside of Cambridge)

Nan was still going on and on about what a mistake it was to break up with The Tutor.

She had broken up with him five years ago.

Nan was still harping on it.

As she explained to Nan, numerous times over the years, she didn't want to get married again, (or for the first time rather). She didn't want to have any more children.

Love Bug was the perfect child. Why have more?

Recognition

Everyone wanted marriage for her in these last years, but it was never what she wanted.

She loved her family, just as it was.

If she was honest, she never wanted four children, as they had once spoken about during the war.

Though, for him, she would have considered it. Perhaps that would have been the danger if their relationship did continue. If she didn't lose him. Perhaps she would have given too much of herself for him. Compromised too much for him. She would have done it happily, for him, but would it have been her in the end?

The Tutor wanted more from her than she could give. He was still a good family friend, and he maintained his scholarly relationship with Love Bug. It was for the best.

Nan, she was sure, was the only one with regrets.

Trying to change the subject, she began to tell Nan of the fight she and Love Bug had the other day.

Her son was perfect in every way, until he wasn't. And as much as she spoiled him, sometimes the answer was no. She wouldn't agree with all of his decisions. This would often result in him running up to his room and slamming the door.

That door slam got on her last nerve.

She always tried to let him make his own decisions in life, within reason.

This day a decision had been made.

He came home and announced that he wanted to join the army.

She had nothing against the army, or any other branch of the miliary. She would be very proud of him, if this is what he wished to do in life. But with his academic standing, she thought he would focus on his studies. All of the top universities were looking at him, not just in the country, but in the world.

"What about school?" she asked.

"I knew you would do this! I knew you wouldn't agree!"

"I'm not saying I don't agree, I just think that with your potential you should focus on Uni."

"Dad was a soldier!"

"That was different. He didn't choose to be a soldier; the war chose for him."

"Well, it's my life, and it's my decision."

"Let's at least discuss your options further, before you make any final decisions," she pleaded.

"This is so typical of you, everything with you is about university. There are other options out there, whether you agree with them or not. You just don't understand! I wish Dad was here instead of you!" he spat.

This silenced her.

And she was not one to be silenced.

She looked at him and then walked out of the house.

He suddenly felt very alone, and scared. She was never silent. It was concerning.

All the times she had blown up in public and told people off, even told him off at times, it was never scary. But this, the silence, was scary.

He knew he had hurt her.

She walked to the phone box and called Gramps, "hi, Gramps, can you pop over and check on Love Bug? We just had a tiff, and I needed to get out to get some air."

"Of course, I'll bring a roast over for supper tonight." he offered.

"That would be grand, ta, Gramps."

Recognition

She walked the length of the river and then sat down on a bench.

It wasn't that she was hurt by his comment. She wished his father was here too. It was just one of those occasions where she thought she was falling short. His father probably would have handled it better. Or, he might have been in perfect agreement with her, she didn't know. But either way, she thought it best he had a man to speak too regarding this decision. She knew he would tell Gramps all about it when he got to the house.

After everything she experienced in the war, she was afraid for her son. The life of a soldier wasn't always the safest life. But she knew she couldn't hold him back if this is what he wants to do.

She sat there for quite some time. Thinking about their life together. It had always been her and her son, and soon, no matter what he decided to do, he would be out of the house, on his own. She couldn't imagine not having him at home with her.

This is the natural order of things. You hope you've raised them well, you care for them and shelter them, and then one day, when they're grown, they leave. Out into the world to make a life for themselves. He grew up too fast, she thought. Where did all the time go?

Suddenly feeling very exhausted, she got up and headed back to the house.

As she opened the door, her son was there to greet her.

He didn't say anything, he just rushed into her arms for a hug.

She didn't get many hugs these days. The teen years – he was too grown up to hug his old Mum.

She held on tight, after a while he tried to pull away, she grabbed on tighter and joked, "no, I'm not letting you go! There's no escaping me now!"

Love Bug laughed, "Mum!"

She released him.

Recognition

"I'm sorry Mum. I didn't mean to say that about Dad."

"It's alright my love; I wish he was here too," she brushed his dark hair out of his eyes.

Love Bug smiled.

"Anyway," she said coming back to her conversation with Nan, "he has an appointment at the recruitment office tomorrow."

Love Bug did join the army. He did his duty, and when the time was right, he returned to his studies. He did it all, in his own time. His mother, as always, was so proud of him.

Over the years, whether in the army or at Uni, he had come home as often as he could. For family occasion, special events, weekend visits with Mum, Nan, and Gramps. He and his mother always remained close, no matter how far he traveled in life.

Elissa Ivy Siegel

Cambridge, 1973

She had never been ill a day in her life. Strong constitution, she'd say.

A few months back, that had changed. The doctor detected something.

She didn't tell anyone, that was her way. She kept it all in, made light of things, and always insisted, "everything will be fine." This time, it wasn't fine. It was terminal.

When it became obvious, when she started to take to her bed, too often and for too long, she told the family.

Nan began to cry.

Gramps reached out and took her hand.

Love Bug left the house.

Recognition

After a time, Gramps went after him.

She looked at Nan, smiling she said, "are you alright, or am I going to have to get up from my sickbed to console you?"

Nan managed a smile, "but you're so young!"

"We know better than most that death has no age requirement."

Nan fell silent.

They heard Gramps and Love Bug returning.

"Why don't you go down and check on Gramps, I have to speak to Love Bug."

"He's not going to take this well."

"I know."

Nan lent over the bed to give her a hug and kiss before she left the room.

Soon, Love Bug was standing in the doorway. He looked scared, afraid to step into the room.

"Come over here, my Love Bug."

He smiled.

"See, I said I'd be calling you Love Bug until you were 30, and here we are."

He sat down next to the bed and took her hand.

"Oh, Mum" he started, and then began to cry.

"I know my love, come here."

He rested his head on her midsection and wept for a long time. She rubbed his back, and brushed his dark hair with her fingers, trying to soothe him. As she had done when he was little, when he felt scared or hurt.

She took his face in her hands, and wiped his tears, dried his face.

"You will be just fine my love, don't be so sad."

Recognition

She went on, "I have had an amazing life, filled with so much love and true joy. You have been my every happiness, my world. I will always be with you, my love."

"I don't want you to go."

"I know. I'm not too crazy about the idea myself."

He smiled.

"I am so proud of you. You have become such an amazing man, kind, and loving, strong, and brilliant, you have done so many wonderful things already, and I know you'll go on to do so much more in life. You are so much like your father, in many ways, and you're very much like me as well – fabulous in every way!" she smiled.

He laughed.

"There's that smile."

"I love you, Mum."

"I love you more."

He leaned in and pulled her into a hug.

"Now, listen to me, there are a few things I want to go over with you."

"Oh, Mum, do we have to go over that now?"

"Yes, come along now. Listen to me, I want you to take care of Nan and Gramps."

"Of Course, I will."

"And I want you to keep the house. Even if you don't want to live in it yourself, let it out to someone who needs it, or let Nan and Gramps move in. Whatever works best for all of you, but I want you to keep the house."

"Ok."

"I love this house. And other than giving you life, it was the one thing your father gave you."

"I know, Mum."

Recognition

"We have had so many wonderful memories here over the years. Also, I plan to haunt it frequently," she joked.

"Mum, ha-ha, that's creepy!"

"As intended," she teased.

They both laughed.

"Now come here my Love Bug and give me a hug."

He curled up next to her and stayed there for a long while in her arms.

Gramps and Nan came into the room, and they spent the rest of the afternoon reminiscing about the good times they have had over the years, the memories of Love Bug's childhood, meeting Gramps all because Mum had yelled at him, the years spent in Nan's flat in London. They laughed and cried, and shared their memories, as they had shared their lives together.

As they were saying good night, one by one, they hugged and kissed her, surrounded by love.

Elissa Ivy Siegel

Love Bug was the last to leave the room.

She held onto him in their embrace, she didn't want to let him go. As they separated, her heart broke a little, and so did his.

"I love you, Mum."

"I love you more."

Alone in her room, she took some things out of her bedside table. Her will, the deed to the house, and their letters. The letters from the war that contained their love. She had never let anyone see these letters, not even when Love Bug would ask question after question about his father. Their letters were too intimate for her to share. Though, now, she thought, Love Bug should have them. His parents love, in words.

As she drifted off to sleep, she could feel him now, almost see him.

A strength at her side.

Recognition

Fifteen
Scotland
1890

The Wedding:

"He looks so handsome, just like you when we got married," she began.

He smiled, "that was ages ago."

"You're still just as handsome."

Even after so many years, he still blushed at the compliment. He reached over and took her hand.

"I like her," she went on, "she'll be good for him."

"You like her because she's just like you."

"She is not."

Recognition

"She's bossy and orders everyone around, everyone apart from you that is."

"That's why I like her."

He smiled.

They fell silent to listen to the couples' vows…

"Do you remember our vows?" he asked.

"Aye, more or less." she teased.

Her Vows, all those years ago:

"My simple Country Analyst, who fell into my life, like an apple obeying the law. I promise to always catch you if you fall. I will be at your side whenever you're in need, whether near or far, you will feel me with you. I see the man you are, and the man you will become, and I am so thrilled and privileged to be able to spend my life with you. I am not blinded by love, I see you fully, the good and the bad, and I love every wonderful aspect of you. I give myself to you completely."

His Vows, all those years ago:

"My Love, it's as if I've known you my whole life. Somehow, you were meant to be my person, my love, my wife. It was written long ago that we would be together, and by some miracle, we found each other. Being with you I am complete. Together, we are whole. No matter how far life takes me, I will always return to you. I will love you every day of my life, and all the other lifetimes to follow."

On this day, their wee ones' wedding day, they felt like that young couple once again.

Remembering honored vows, and the days that filled their marriage.

They walked into the hall at the main house.

Recognition

Cook has been working all week for the occasion.

The feast was magnificent. The guests were having a wonderful time. The newlyweds were beaming with happiness. And the family were together again… well, most of them.

"I wish Mum and Da' could be here," she said to her husband.

"I know Love, we all miss them terribly."

Mother had passed nearly six years ago, and Da' followed her three years later.

She knew it pained her youngest not to have them here. She looked at her sons. They were all together congregating in the corner of the hall talking and catching up on each other's lives.

It has been a long while since they were all together.

Their eldest had gone off to travel the world as soon as he was able. He would work odd jobs, and keep traveling from country to country, continent to continent. He would always write home and tell them of his adventures.

Their second eldest was a professor at St. Andrews. With a cottage by the sea, he had settled into academia very happily.

Their third son was working with artists and sculptors in Edinburgh. Although painting was always his main interest, he had taken up sculpting in the last few years and had created and sold some amazing pieces.

The three of them came home as often as they were able. And the family visited St. Andrews and Edinburgh at every chance.

Finally, their wee one, the youngest, married today, and now living in the house he grew up in. Though he was not wee any longer, growing larger than all three of this brothers. He was more and more like his father with each passing day. He had even taken his old job, surveying the lands.

"He is the very spit of you," she always reminded her husband.

All of their sons were very content with the lives they had chosen for themselves.

She and her husband moved to the big house after Mum and Da' passed.

They kept Cook on at the house, of course, she was family, after all.

Later that night, after all the guests had gone, the new couple went off on their honeymoon, their other three sons went to stay at their family home and Cook retired for the night. She and The Analyst sat down in the sitting room.

"Do you remember that party Mother had, when we were courting?" he began.

"Aye, The Soiree."

He smiled, "yes, the soiree; I very nearly didn't make it back in time."

"Back in time for what?"

"Back in time for you."

"Your timing was perfect."

She teasingly went on, "mind you, Bachelor #10, or maybe it was #11, was in the running for a while. Mother would have married me off the next day if I had showed any real interest in him."

"Yes, Mother didn't like me much in the beginning."

"She was very happy to see the back of you," she smiled, "but you grew on her after a while... over the years there were times I thought she loved you even more than me."

He smiled, "we had our nightly talks, she warmed up shortly after those began."

"What did you two speak about all those years?"

"You and Da'."

She smiled.

Recognition

"In any case," he went on, "if it wasn't for Da' I would have missed the soiree completely. Leaving you in the clutches of Bachelor #10, or #11."

"What do you mean?"

"Da' sent me a letter."

"What!?" she asked

"He sent me a letter."

"What did it say?"

"He wrote to say that if I was serious about you, then I had better get back here and go to that soiree. He explained that Mother was matchmaking again, and that our long time apart had been hard on you. Da' asked me never to tell anyone he had written to me. He said if I truly loved you, I'd better get to that party, no matter what. And so, I did."

She sat for a moment thinking about Da'. Dear old Da', always trying to give his daughter everything she wanted or needed in life.

He went on, "I was commissioned to stay on assignment for at least another year when that letter arrived. I had to move heaven and earth to get back for that soiree."

"Another year!"

"Yes, it would have been another year before I could get back this way. I would have lost you."

"You wouldn't have lost me," she said, reaching over and taking his hand.

"Could you have done another year of letters? Nothing but words between us all that time?"

She thought back to when they were courting, "we had a lot more between us, it wasn't just words. We had silence. We had distance. Not just then, but for much of our married life. And we had so much love between us that it filled the silence, and it bridged the gap of distance."

He brought her hand to his lips and kissed it.

Recognition

They sat hand in hand, thinking about their marriage, their life together, their children. It had been a beautiful day. It had been a beautiful life. A life lived in love.

Finally, she said, "look who turned out to be the matchmaker after all!"

He added, "Mother would have been furious!"

They laughed.

Still hand in hand, she stood up, "Come on my lover, let's go to bed, and <u>not</u> sleep a wink."

He looked at her, smiling, he led the way.

Elissa Ivy Siegel

Sixteen

Boston

1775

She didn't sleep much on the park bench. At a very early hour, she returned to the barracks to get a few of her things. No one was there. The place looked abandoned.

She grabbed her documents, and some items of clothing. She packed the dress, for England, but she dressed as a boy this day. The bald head and severe bruising did somewhat clash with a hoop skirt. There would be time in England to step back into her life as a girl, as a woman.

She left and made her way to the morgue.

The Caretaker wasn't there, it was too early. In some ways, she was grateful. He wouldn't want to see her like this. After placing two letters in The Caretakers letter box, she made her way to the pier.

The British soldier was already there, bright and early.

They boarded the ship and settled in for a long journey.

As they set sail, she remained at the aft, looking at her home, her country. She stared at the apple cart on the pier until it was out of view.

Surrounded by ocean, she returned to the British soldier.

"Let me take a look at your wounds," he said as he saw her approach.

"I'm fine."

"Nothing is broken, that's true, but you look far from fine."

She let him examine her wounds.

Bruised ribs, swelling, sore back, deep cuts, some that would scar.

They sat out on the deck after he was finished.

"So how are you the lucky one to win a journey back to England?" she asked.

Recognition

"I was already on my way home. Escorting you was an added bonus."

"It seems to me the war is kicking off; wouldn't you be better suited here?"

"I've been commissioned by The Crown, to act as a personal physician. I'm going back to complete my studies and attend to the Royal family." He went on, "If I'm honest, I'm not much of a soldier."

"You're strong enough, you pulled that Redcoat off of me with great ease."

"I am strong, and I can fight, but I'd much rather heal and help people, not hurt them."

(Swoon)

That is the most wonderful thing she thinks she has ever heard.

He continued, "you're a pretty good fighter yourself. That Redcoat is our strongest, and best. And you completely took him out of commission, he isn't fit to fight now."

"Really? It felt as if I barely made him flinch."

"You shattered his kneecap."

"I thought I did, but he didn't go down. He didn't give any sign of being injured; he is a beast."

"He was The British Commander's best soldier. As your man is The General's best soldier."

"He is not my man."

"In any case, you fought well. And left an impression."

"Did I?"

"Your general spoke on your behalf. He explained to The Commander what an asset you have been, as a Patriot. He talked them down from the charge of treason. And encouraged The Commander to put you to good use."

Recognition

"Good use?"

"To work with us, in England."

"Fighting, as a boy?" she asked.

"Not fighting, no; And you can be whoever you want to be, but it is not necessary to remain a boy, if you do not wish. It will mostly be an office position. You were quite good at obtaining information and strategic planning. The General made us see that we could use your assistance."

She was pleased The General spoke on her behalf. He was a good man.

"What made you start dressing like a boy?" he asked.

"I felt so unsafe in this world of men that I had to become one in order to survive," she said simply, though it was anything but.

He looked at her with such sincere concern, it was touching.

"It's ok," She said seeing his expression. "I was good at it, as you've pointed out. It wasn't a bad life these last years."

"What will your Patriots do without you now?" he asked.

"Oh, they will be fine I expect. The British are no match for them," she teased.

He smiled. "Maybe. Especially as you've taken out The Commander's best man."

"War isn't won by one man alone, or one woman for that matter."

He nodded.

"Do you know, I'd be quite happy if I never had to fight again," she confessed.

"When we arrive in England, I will be your main contact. I'll help you settle into the job, and the housing we have set up for you. As you settle in, if there is anything you need, you can reach out to me," he informed her.

"So, you'll be the one looking after me?"

"We will look after each other."

Recognition

(Does this guy ever put a word wrong?)

"Thank you," she said, sincerely.

The two letters she left for The Caretaker:

The first letter was for The Caretaker. It explained what had happened, who she was, and how she was being sent back to England. She left him the address that The Commander had given her for her place in London. And she left the second letter, a letter for him, her Patriot.

The letter to her Patriot was an apology, an explanation. She tried to express it all in these words, but she knew the words would fall short. They wouldn't be enough to make amends. But she had to try.

Shortly after arriving in London, The Caretakers first letter would arrive. It would be the first of many letters between them in the years to come. He informed her that he had passed her letter onto her Patriot. The Patriot didn't say anything, and The Caretaker never saw him again. Though, she would always ask for him in her letters over the years.

Still no word? No sighting? Nothing?

Although she would never hear from him again, she would not forget him.

Her friend. Her family. Her Patriot.

Seventeen

The United States of America

2022

The friend she traveled to the UK with called her one night.

They chatted about their lives and generally caught up after not speaking for a few months. Peoples' lives get busy. They could go months without speaking to one another, but as friends, they knew each other is always there for them when needed.

It had been a very good year for her. She entered this year with many intentions, and she nearly ticked all the boxes. She had lost nearly 65 pounds, she was entering fitness challenges and led wellness talks, she traveled extensively, work was going very well. She intended to foster a certain balance in her life. And for the most part, all things were on point.

Singletons have their shit together. On the off chance that their shit isn't together, they work very hard to make it so. Determination in all things.

She started to tell him about a fitness seminar she was recently asked to attend as a guest speaker.

She told him of her icebreaker, during her talk.

Addressing the seminar participants:

"It wasn't easy, my fitness journey took a lot of work and dedication - though the process is actually very simple," she stood up to speak and started counting down a checklist with the fingers on her right hand. "I essentially got rid of a few things that needed to be cut from my lifestyle:

1. I cut out sugar.
2. I cut out processed foods.

Recognition

3. I cut out high caloric beverages.
4. I cut out toxic men and relationships."

The crowd laughed.

"You laugh, but that was 200lbs of excessive weight right there!" she added.

They laughed again.

"Thank you so much for finding my disastrous love life so humorous," she smiled.

More laugher.

She continued to tell the group about her fitness journey, and her most recent weight loss success now in her mid-40's.

They were an amazing group, and she still hears from the participants today regarding their own progress and successes.

She came back to her phone conversation.

"200lbs of excess weight, that's hilarious!" he said.

Then he asked, "did you ever hear from that guy?"

"What guy?" she asked. She knew what guy; she was trying to play it cool.

"The one who disappeared, and never spoke to you again."

"No. He was never to be heard from again," she confessed.

Her friend seemed frustrated by the idea that he never got in touch.

"What on earth could have happened?" he asked.

She reminded him that he had been with his partner for 30 years, dating and meeting people these days was very different. Ghosting, albeit spineless, was a very common occurrence.

He kept pressing, "but why!?"

"I don't know my friend, we can speculate several different scenarios, but in the end, I can't tell you why. Only he knows why, and he's not speaking to me now."

Recognition

She went on, "I promise, if I ever find out, if I ever get an explanation, you'll be the first to know," she was touched that he was upset on her behalf, he was a good friend.

After thinking about it, her friend concluded, "people are such assholes. You should forget all about him, he isn't worth it."

What she never told anyone, is that she didn't want to forget him. She didn't want to let go. It wasn't that she wouldn't or couldn't move on, she had already done that.

But forgetting him felt wrong somehow.

She thought about him for a moment; was it possible to love someone you barely knew?

Was it possible for love to grow in his silence?

The difficulty with being silenced is that it brings you to the point where you do not want to speak any longer.

You tire of struggling to be heard.

The anger you felt over being silenced subsides, and you comply.

"As I said," she continued, "it was nothing." (It was something.) "I thought there was a mutual recognition between us, but I was wrong. It was all in my head. Nothing but a fantasy."

"I'm sorry, Hun," her friend consoled.

"It's ok."

    We will find each other in the next life, she thought.

Eighteen

Ireland

1622

She saw a pack of boys beating up a smaller boy, who appeared to be on his own.

They all looked to be around her age, 10 or there abouts.

One of the pack threw a punch and boxed his ears.

She got that look on her face whenever witnessing an injustice.

Her brow would crinkle, her deep blue eyes would narrow, and her face would shine crimson.

"As if she has the Devil in her", her Da' used to say.

"Let's just be thankful she uses her temper for good", her Mum would remind him. (Usually)

She charged at the pack of boys at full force, knocking one of them to the ground. Hard.

She grabbed a fist full of the culprit's hair and started walloping him.

The other bullies ran off.

Feeling as though she had made her point, she let her victim go.

He ran off in the direction of the others.

She stood up brushing the dirt off her dress and started to compose herself.

She looked at the boy they had set upon.

He had a pleasing face.

She stood there for a moment, taking him in.

"Are you alright?" she asked.

"Yes, I'm fine. Thank you for chasing them off."

She looked at him, longer this time, and said, "I think we're going to be great friends, stick with me and I will protect you."

The boy smiled.

She was like that. She would look at someone and decide in an instant if this was someone she wanted to invite into her life forever or dismiss them with the flick of her wrist.

Recognition

"Do you want to play Pirates?" she asked.

"Ok"

"Just so long as I get to be The Captain of the ship," she added.

This time the boy looked at her, taking her in.

He smiled, and wisely answered, "ok."

She grinned.

Then turning to him, she reached up to tend to the wound on his ear.

"This is going to need stitching."

The Beginning.

Elissa Ivy Siegel

Recognition

Afterword & Acknowledgements

(Also, a good read, if you're so inclined.)

Thank you for taking the time to read my story.

It was a great pleasure bringing these characters to life on the page.

It started with an idea based on a connection. A connection that came from the briefest of encounters, and yet, I couldn't help but feel that it meant more than it did.

Why do we feel so drawn to people we have only just met?

Someone you've only known for an instant, fleeting.

Where did this sense of connection come from when you never truly knew each other?

I thought the idea of past lives was an endearing way to explore and express these connections.

Recognizing another's soul, time and time again.

If our souls can carry-on from lifetime to lifetime; so too can our love, and our scars.

Elissa Ivy Siegel

My dearly departed family are echoed in these pages.
Mother and Da' honor my parents with a distinct accuracy.
Nan, created from memories of my own Nana, and a mix of prominent female family friends.
Gramps shares similarities with my pal Al, our close family friend who was like a second dad to me, and a friend to all.
Love Bug, who was nearly a reality in life, but alas never came to be. I never thought I wanted children, but it was incredibly fulfilling being 'Mum,' if only on the page.

A special thanks to my friends who appeared throughout the story, my UK travel companion, The Scotsman, the past relationships that built the characters, and set the scene.
Everyone who helped this story come to light. Mel, who took the story and made it a book!
My friends who read and re-read copy, giving feedback, loads of praise, and endless support.
Vin, Rusty, John, Greg, Kelly, Livy, Geri, Carolyn.

Recognition

(In truth, you cannot trust them - they're biased; they think everything I do is amazing!)

To you, the reader, even if you thought this story was complete rubbish, and your copy is now propping up a wobbly table leg; I still appreciate you giving it a read.

Finally, a genuinely, heartfelt, Thank You, to my simple Country Analyst.
He who lit a spark, and nothing more.
(Though, I thought it was something more.)

Elissa Ivy Siegel

www.ingramcontent.com/pod-product-compliance
Lightning Source LLC
Chambersburg PA
CBHW030431010526
44118CB00011B/587